Praise for An Actor Rehearses

"With all of the old wives' tales about actors and general skepticism surrounding the craft, Hlavsa single-handedly provides a compelling, complimentary argument for the difficulties and triumphs of the profession of acting."

—Molly Smith, Artistic Director, Arena Stage

"Hlavsa leads the reader through the rehearsal process step by step, with such thoroughness and clarity that his book cannot help but provide an actor with both insight and encouragement."

—M. Burke Walker, Founding Artistic Director,
The Empty Space Theatre

"Essential. This book will go near the top of my 'must read' booklist for actors and directors."

—Mark Jenkins, Head, MFA Professional Actor Training
Program and MFA Directing Program, University
of Washington School of Drama

"This book can be used as a how-to manual for the beginning actor, as well as a source of replenishment and inspiration for the grizzled veteran. As a director, actor, and acting teacher, I will call upon Mr. Hlavsa's wisdom often."

—Tony Pasqualini, Actor, Director, and Founder,
Freehold Theatre, Studio and Lab

An Actor
Rehearses

An Actor Rehearses

What to Do When—and Why

David Hlavsa

**ALLWORTH
PRESS**
NEW YORK

10 09 08 07 06   5 4 3 2 1

Published by Allworth Press
An imprint of Allworth Communications, Inc.
10 East 23rd Street, New York, NY 10010

Cover design by Derek Bacchus
Interior design by Robin Black, Blackbird Creative LLC
Page composition/typography by: Integra Software Services, Pvt. Ltd., Pondicherry, India
Cover photo credit: A digital image, taken by Gerry Goldstein, of Terry Greiss and Damon Scranton of the Irondale Ensemble Project, in rehearsal. © Gerry Goldstein

ISBN-13: 978-1-58115-462-7
ISBN-10: 1-58115-462-3

Library of Congress Cataloging-in-Publication Data:

Hlavsa, David.
    An actor rehearses: what to do when—and why / David Hlavsa.
       p.   cm.
    ISBN-13: 978-1-58115-462-7 (pbk.)
    ISBN-10: 1-58115-462-3 (pbk.)
1. Theater rehearsals.   I. Title.

PN2071.R45H53 2006
792.02'8—dc22

2006026629

Printed in Canada

Dedication

To my wife, Lisa Holtby, and my son, Benjamin.
My hearts.

Acknowledgments

I grew up in the theatre. That's not to say that I came from a theatrical family or started acting at a particularly young age; I didn't. But a good amount of what I've managed to learn about relationships, community, hard work, expressiveness, honesty, responsibility, and so on, I owe to working on plays.

Much of what I have to offer as a teacher and director comes from my own acting and directing teachers (in order of appearance: Jordan Hornstein, Paul Zimet, Alan and Carol MacVey, Jack Sydow, Bob Loper, Sue-Ellen Case, Paul Hostetler, and Barry Witham). They taught me what I know about the craft, but more importantly, they insisted that I get my own act together. Following their advice, I've found that whatever work I've done on myself—trying to become a more effective leader, a more loving husband and father, a kinder person—has helped me to mature as an actor and director as well.

In this regard, a lot of the people who have helped me to get better at what I do for a living are not at all involved with theatre. I owe a great deal to Bob and Judith Wright; many of the techniques and exercises in this book—particularly in the sections dealing with emotion and consciousness—are inspired by their work at Chicago's School of Exceptional Living. My fellow travelers and good friends, Paul Fischburg, Danny Geiger, Todd Jacobs, Denis Martynowych, Joe Shirley, and Carl Woestwin have also been powerful teachers.

This book would not have been possible without the support of Saint Martin's University (especially my colleagues on the Faculty Development

Committee, who granted me a sabbatical to write it) and of my wife, Lisa Holtby, a fine writer and teacher (check out her book at *www.lisaholtby.com*), a savvy businesswoman, and a very smart editor.

Many thanks to my students, especially Brandon Barney, Beth McCoy, Christian Pearson, and Craig Woodworth, for "test-driving" this material in acting class and rehearsal; to David Robinson, Meg Patterson, Irwin Appel, Annette Romano, and Dick and Vivi Hlavsa for reading early drafts of the book and providing much-needed encouragement and criticism; to David Price, Mark Glubke of Back Stage Books, and Linda Konner for advice on publishing; and to Nicole Potter-Talling, Jessica Rozler, and Tad Crawford at Allworth Press for seeing the good in my manuscript and for making it better.

I'm sure there are other people I should acknowledge. New acting exercises and rehearsal techniques spread through the profession like viruses, hitting everyone at once and mutating rapidly; it's often hard to say where and when we've picked them up. I have tried to be scrupulous about giving credit, but I'm afraid this book is bound to contain a measure of unconscious pilferage. My apologies to anyone I've slighted.

Contents

Introduction: Why Are You on Stage?

IT'S THE FIRST DAY OF REHEARSAL. After all the work, all the planning that's already gone into the show, after all the stress and excitement of auditions, after the actors, the designers, the stage managers, the director have all arranged their lives to be here, it's time for us to get down to actually rehearsing the play. At last, everyone is gathered in one room. People are excited, nervous—even a little giddy.

Happily, there's a ritual to follow on the first day: you sit around a big table, and you read the play aloud. So that's what we do. People start to read the words. Everyone flips pages in unison. Some people sound convincing; some don't. Some plunge right in; some seem more reserved. Some get laughs. Somebody does a scene on the verge of tears. As he reads one of his longer speeches from the play, one actor thinks, "I was born to play this role," while the guy sitting next to him is thinking, "I could do better than that." The director sits very still, listening intently, trying to stop asking herself whether the leading actor she's cast is really right for the part. Two actors, a man and a woman who have never met before, are playing a love scene. The script tells us the characters are half-dressed, kissing each other passionately. She sneaks a glance at him, feels no attraction whatsoever, and wonders how on earth she's going to pull this off. By the time we've finished reading through the play, people are still excited, but a kind of sobriety has descended upon the room.

Now what do we do?

We're all holding a copy of this *text*. How are we supposed to take the words on the page and turn them into a live performance? Everyone's aware that we've got a lot of work to do. But where do we start? What step comes first? Then what? Even if we've all done this before, it seems as though it's going to take a minor miracle—or perhaps a series of minor miracles—to get from here to there.

In part, this book is about the *sequence* of the actor's work, otherwise known as the actor's *process*, starting before the first readthrough and continuing through the rehearsals, opening, performances, and closing night of the show. If you know what to expect at any given phase of rehearsal, you can work more efficiently, investing your full attention in each discrete task. You know what you need to do first, what challenges you are likely to encounter in the middle, and what parts of the task to save until the end. It's a matter of putting one foot in front of the other, but it's anything but pedestrian. Having a sense of the process can spare you a great deal of frustration and prepare the way for extraordinary discoveries.

Further, if you can recognize when you're ready to move forward in the sequence and when you're *not* ready, it can help keep you from succumbing to one of the actor's biggest temptations: going for immediate results. More often than not, rushing or skipping over the process leads to a performance composed chiefly of clichés, generalities, and superficial gestures. It's not that good things *never* happen quickly. Sometimes, you just *respond* instinctually—to the words, the situation, the other actors—and you do something that's moving, theatrical, brilliant. If you're lucky, your instincts are leading you in the right direction. But sometimes the choices an actor makes in these leaps forward are not the right ones for the long term; sometimes, they're flat-out wrong for the play. More importantly, most often, you can't repeat or recreate them. If you don't know how you got there, how are you going to get there again?

In a sense, your job as an actor in rehearsal is to get up in front of the director and the other actors and stumble around until you can find your footing. Sometimes making progress is anything but graceful, so it's nice to be able to recognize when you're taking baby steps in the right direction and celebrate small victories as well as large ones. If you know what to expect, you may find it easier to be gentle and patient with yourself on the tough days—the days when you suspect your character is hateful and completely outside of your grasp, days when you're mortified that this show will *ever* be in front of an audience. You can say, "Oh, *this* place," heave a deep sigh, and get back to work.

I try to keep things as simple as possible in rehearsal, and I've tried to describe them simply here. Otherwise the task at hand can seem overwhelming, and then it's hard to get anything done. In general, the work proceeds from the simple to the complex, from the obvious to the subtle. We start with what the playwright has given us, what the character outwardly expresses, with the words, the surface behavior, and work our way downward, *deeper.*

Imagine for the moment that the character you are going to play is an actual person, and you want to get to know him—I mean, *really* know him, really get close to him. I doubt you'd expect any quick results; in fact, I suspect you'd be a little squeamish about getting in there right away. You'd want to at least get *acquainted* first.

So you start with surfaces and first impressions. What he looks like. What he says. What he does for a living. The way he behaves in public. You also have reactions to him, emotional responses, some of which you're aware of and some of which you may not be. Given that our first impressions of others are inevitably colored by our own past experiences and prejudices, some of your initial ideas about him may be accurate while others are wildly off the mark. Odds are, even this early in the game, you've decided whether you like him or not.

But even if you don't like him, you keep on trying to learn about him. Eventually, you come to learn more about what he likes and dislikes, his reactions to people, places, things. You see him in the context of the people he chooses to be with—and the people he's stuck with. You start to notice some quirks in his behavior, things that seem to indicate that he's not telling you everything.

You may have thought you had him figured out, but then he does something that completely contradicts your theory about him. Maybe you felt superior to him (or intimidated by him), but now you don't anymore. Mostly, you're puzzled. You realize that, even though you know him a little, you're still mostly strangers. You may have gathered the plain facts, but you're still somehow at a distance; you're still on the outside.

What will it take to get closer?

Just as in the maturing of a marriage or the formation of a close friendship, the process of rehearsing a role proceeds from surface to core. The words, the behaviors we first encounter in reading the script are most often a social veneer, a mask covering the character's thoughts, emotions, drives, desires, delusions, plans, and so on. To complicate the task, the character's inner life may be as much a mystery to him as it is to the actor. Characters lie. All the time. To each other, to the audience, and to themselves. Sometimes, the circumstances of the play will be such that the character is forced to express himself fully, but often the audience only gets the merest peek inside. The façade cracks; the mask slips. Think of Willy Loman in *Death of a Salesman*; he would literally rather die than admit to himself or others what is really going on inside him. One reason characters lie is that there would be no drama without deceit. But more importantly, they are deceivers because that's what we all do. Our inner life is mostly contained. Even those who know us best can know only a fraction of what's going on underneath, and often we couldn't tell them because we don't know either.

A further complication: when we get under the mask, there's often another mask beneath that one. Layer upon layer, we cover one emotion with another. Most often we do this without any conscious intent or even awareness that we are doing so. It happens in an instant. Something scares me, but without even realizing that I'm afraid, I camouflage the fear with anger. Someone says something hurtful to me, and I make a joke. What brought me to that response? In that moment, I couldn't tell you. I haven't even noticed that I felt pain, got angry, considered hurting him back, imagined that he might be mad and retaliate, got scared, considered my options, and decided to use humor to avoid a confrontation. All I'm conscious of is the result: making light of the situation.

Not surprisingly, the characters playwrights have written for us often suffer from the same difficulties. For example, at the core a character may be terrified, even though very little of that fear shows through. If you're playing Iago, your first access to his emotional life is almost certainly through what makes him angry. But if you only work at the level of anger, sooner or later, you'll probably start to notice that your choices are starting to become stale and your performance cartoonish. Once you've got the outer layers, how much richer to explore how Iago may be terrified of—and perhaps even in love with—Othello.

Working your way inward by stages—thinking of the character as an actual human being you are coming to know—helps you to create a multifaceted, dimensional character and to prepare you for the mental, physical, and emotional complexity of playing that character for an audience. However, in preparing to perform a role, each time we hit a new level, it is crucial to assess the work—to recognize that the character is *not* in fact a living person we are seeking to know, but a fictional construct. If we take a step back and evaluate the likely effect of each choice on the audience, we may come to see that some of what has helped the actor "feel closer" to the character may not serve the play.

In performance, the actor lives two lives at once. She is both the character and herself. She moves back and forth between experiencing the life of the character from the inside and—as if she were standing outside herself—monitoring the effectiveness of her own performance. She plays intimate moments so loud that her words can be clearly understood in the back row. She alternates between responding spontaneously to the other actors and, in order to build intensity gradually rather than peaking too soon, carefully calibrating her emotional reactions.

Your rehearsal process needs to be one that prepares you to inhabit these simultaneous, seemingly contradictory realities. The different phases of the work described here are designed to help you switch back and forth between feeling and thinking, inside and outside, details and big picture.

Of course, these modes of working aren't really contradictory. They support, inform, and overlap one another. So each time we switch to a new mode of working, you'll notice that I'm insisting on being mindful of its opposite. Indeed any time you concentrate on one mode, it's useful to notice how the opposite practically forces its way in. Thinking, for example, is not a dispassionate activity—good ideas *feel right*. Similarly, there's no such thing as emotion without thought; humans are conscious animals—we don't just feel; we have thoughts *about* what we feel. How you move dictates how you feel and vice versa. Often the best way to evoke an emotion is to try to suppress it. Want to get a sense of the whole character? Start with details. And so on.

Playing opposites in rehearsal not only trains you to sustain the actor's dual role in performance, it honors the complexity of what you're trying to accomplish: that is, impersonating another human being. Learn to love contradictions. At the very least, they will keep you from getting *stale*.

Once the show is in front of an audience, your job changes radically; the challenges of performance are of a different order than those of rehearsal. Nonetheless, the tasks you face and the issues you encounter at the beginning, middle, and end of a run are, for the most part, sequential and predictable. Here too, it helps if you know what's coming, recognize each phase as it arrives and have concrete steps to take. And it helps if you know how to keep experimenting with alternatives, oppositions, contradictions, because the moment you think you've got your performance nailed, you're dead.

You know the euphoria of giving a good performance: everything flows effortlessly and every choice you make is honest, clear, emotionally engaged. The rest of the cast is on fire. The audience is enthralled; they are right with you. You think, "I wish every show was like this."

I believe it is just possible for you to play an entire run of a show, even a long run, in which you attain this state every single time, sometimes from first line to final curtain. This is a radical notion. Most of us believe that some shows are bound to be "off" nights. Sometimes every effort we make just seems to sink the play, the audience, and us into a sump of painful lethargy. What is worse, these off nights seem to have no particular pattern, and sometimes no identifiable cause. Most of us believe that off nights come like bad weather—nothing we can do. But if you know what to expect and how to deal with it, you have a far better chance of establishing rapport with your character, with your fellow actors and with your audience.

Your chances are even better if you know, not just *what* to do, but also *why* you are doing it. If you want to do a good show for your opening night, your twentieth night, your closing night audience, I think it will be helpful to talk about the reasons we're in theatre in the first place. If part of rehearsing a role is figuring out the character's intentions, part of sustaining the role in performance has to do with examining and evaluating our *own* motives. In rehearsal, we do well to select the strongest most playable, most engaging motives for our character; likewise we have a better chance of being consistent, inspired performers, if we anchor each night, each show, in *our* strongest motives.

Ultimately, this book is about acting for a higher purpose. What is it we want for the audience? What is it we want for ourselves? What do we stand for in the world? What are we committed to? What is important about playing this role, on this night, for this audience?

Most of us start acting because it's a rush. Rehearsal is an intense communal experience. We fall in love with the other actors in the cast: we're part of the joint enterprise of doing something complex and difficult under pressure. As people do in wartime, we form intense attachments. Then we put the show in front of an audience, they laugh, we score, people clap for us. Then we do a terrible show, and everyone's miserable. Then we do a good show, and everyone's happy again. The run of the show ends. We rip down the set with power tools. People get drunk at the cast party. Everyone comes down with a cold. Then off to the next show. Start over.

I'm not going to say there's anything wrong with this. There are far worse things to be hooked on. But the difference between being a theatre junkie and using theatre as an expression of a higher purpose is analogous to the difference between drinking wine to get loaded and drinking it as part of Holy Communion. Why drink spirits when what you really want is Spirit?

When you ground your reason for performing in a higher purpose, it not only improves your acting, it starts to manifest in other areas besides the theatre. Learning how to become a better actor is one way to become a better person. Better in the sense of kinder to others, but also in the sense of more functional, more intentional, more centered, more openhearted, more conscious, more *alive.*

CHAPTER 1

Before Rehearsals Start: Step Up to the Plate

A LOT OF ACTORS, even diligent ones, come to the first rehearsal under-prepared. Legitimately concerned about fixing on an interpretation that will turn out to be in conflict with the director's vision, they hold off on educating themselves about the play and the role before heading into rehearsals. Yes, you want to start rehearsals with a blank slate, but being open to ideas is not the same as coming in ignorant. As a family friend used to say, "You don't want to be so open-minded that your brains fall out." Most often there's some period of time between the day you find out you've been cast in a show and the day you go into rehearsal. Let's talk about how to use that time to advantage.

Most actors follow instructions well; when I'm directing, they're dutiful about trying to give me "what I want." Others I've worked with have strong ideas about what they ought to be doing—which is fine—but they resist direction. And then there are some—the ones I want to work with again and again—who come to rehearsals ready to *collaborate*.

What makes an actor a collaborator? First, he does his work, keeps his focus, and brings loads of energy to rehearsal. Second, he's always got lots of ideas for things to try (and he'll try anything), but he's not so attached to any of them that he can't let go. The reason he always brings lots of ideas is: that's the actor's job. The reason he's able to let go of ideas is: that's *also* the actor's job. He recognizes that the director is ultimately responsible for interpreting the play, for choosing what will be best for the production and for guiding his performance. I recognize he's got his job to do, and I try to give him what he needs, which often means staying out of his way.

Neither of us is trying to take over the other's job. We're engaged in a common cause. All through the rehearsal period, there's a mutually satisfying, ongoing conversation—sometimes spoken, sometimes not—about which of the choices he's making are going to work best for the show. Some of the ideas he brings in don't work. But even those that don't work are usually *good ideas*. Why? In part, because he's done his homework: he knows the play.

It can take some discipline for an actor to spend time surveying the whole landscape of a play. Most of us want to rush in there with the highlighter and mark our territory. But think of it this way: you're part of a group effort to realize something that's larger than the sum of individual performances. Of course, before rehearsals start, your primary obligation is to do your homework with respect to your own role. However, if you can manage it, start by trying to come to terms with the play as a *whole*.

You'll save everyone a lot of time in rehearsal if you have some sense of where your character fits into the larger scheme of things and how the play *works*. Plays have a certain mechanical aspect to them; the playwright has deliberately constructed her work to function a certain way in the theatre. If you've studied the mechanics of the play beforehand—if you know what makes it go—you'll start rehearsals with a better sense of what will serve the production. Your choices will be smarter and your false starts fewer.

Just how much pre-rehearsal time you can spend focusing on the play as a whole depends on how much time you *have*. You can't do everything. Use common sense. Prioritize. If rehearsals start in a week, and you are playing a schizophrenic with mid-stage Parkinson's and a Latvian accent, best skip the thoughtful analysis. Give the play a quick read and scan the section below on researching the physical demands of the character. Then go get help.

But if you've got some time, here are some ways you can get to know your character *in the context of the whole play*:

First Impressions

Before you dive in, get yourself *ready* to read the play for the first time. (If you've already read it, pretend you haven't.) You're going to bring to the task as much attention and as little agenda as you can. This will be your last opportunity to experience the play as a member of the audience might experience it, to be in suspense about what happens next, to take an immediate liking to one character while instantly disliking another, to be astonished by what the characters do or fail to do. If you concentrate on *noticing* how the play works on you now, then you can remind yourself of these first impressions periodically throughout the rehearsal process, especially as you approach opening night.

Unlike your opening night audience, who will have the benefit of (we hope and trust) a fully realized production, right now you can only experience the play through the words on the page in front of you. This places great demands on your imagination; you are asking yourself to envision without being able to actually see, to listen closely without being able to hear. In order to really take in the play, you're going to need to be exceptionally alert.

When I first read a play, I have to fight to keep track of the basics: which character is which, what the relationships are, and what's going on. Unless I've carved out a generous amount of time and I've spent a few minutes relaxing my body and calming my mind, I have a hard time bringing my full focus to what I am reading. But it's worth the effort; an inattentive first reading leads to half-baked first impressions.

Maybe you're not as restless a person as I am. Still, you might want to try setting up your first reading as kind of ritual. *Consecrate* some time—or at least make sure you're choosing a time when your mind is sharp and distractions will be minimal. Don't over-caffeinate. Hydrate. Do some yoga. If you find it helps your concentration to go sit in a café or in the library, go, get out of the house. Turn off your cell phone. Bring a favorite pen and a notebook you have chosen especially for working on this play—from now until the play closes, you'll keep them with you to jot down ideas as they occur to you.

Now, you've done all you reasonably can do to prepare to read, so go easy. As you read, pretend you haven't been cast in a particular role, and give your attention to the whole play. Try to involve your senses in what's going on; notice if images or sounds arise in your mind, but don't obsess about seeing or hearing everything. If your mind wanders, if you find you're losing track of who is who, if you find yourself skimming or skipping, go back a couple of pages and get yourself oriented. Read at a moderate, comfortable pace. When you're done, I'd suggest going for a short walk so you can absorb what you just read. Then sit down and make some notes.

What you're after is "free-writing," that is, unedited raw thoughts, ideas, impressions, feelings, and questions about the play, set down as quickly as you physically can. As a teacher of mine once put it, you want to find the shortest distance between your brain and the page. Your writing doesn't have to be pretty, well phrased, original or even particularly coherent. In fact, beware of well-turned phrases; you don't want to be clever right now. You may contradict yourself. You may repeat yourself. You may start in one direction, then veer abruptly off somewhere else. You're not trying to reach a conclusion. All you're doing is collecting. Keep it simple.

Write until you need a break. With your notebook near at hand, do something else for a while (something routine and physical works best for me: exercise, wash the dishes, etc.), and then write some more.

Reading and Re-Reading

Over the next few days, read the play as many times as you can and set aside more time to make notes. As I'm gathering raw material in this way, I find it helps to have two basic questions in the back of my mind: "What strikes me?" and "What's weird?"

WHAT STRIKES ME? What stands out? Who do I like? Who don't I like? What's funny? What's ironic? What about the play evokes strong feelings in me?

There's a good chance that most of what strikes you is going to strike your opening night audience, too. It pays to notice what's having an impact on you now, because, even as the rehearsal process sensitizes you to the play's finer points, if you're not careful, it can numb you to the obvious. Does your heart go out to a character? Does a character irritate you? (Especially useful to notice if he happens to be *your* character.) Is there a character you identify with? (Especially interesting if she's *not* the one you are playing.) Is the play suspenseful? Where does the tension increase or let up? Are there parts you find distressing? Sad? Clever? Funny? Outrageous? What attracts you? What repels you? Above all, what moves you? What *excites* you?

WHAT'S WEIRD? Is there anything in the play that seems out of place? What doesn't make sense? What do I find mysterious, unusual, extreme?

Noticing what's weird gives you an idea of what things you, the director, and the rest of the cast will need to come to terms with about the play. How come Othello is so easily duped by Iago? Doesn't calling the play *Death of a Salesman* kind of give away the ending? What's Hedda so upset about? What's up with all those toasters? Keep in mind that coming to terms with the play's mysteries and oddities may not mean solving them. Or it may mean solving them for yourself but not for the audience. We come to the theatre to be astonished. We want extraordinary events, even if they happen within the lives of seemingly mundane characters. Preserve the weird. It will serve you later.

As you continue to read and write about the play as a whole, see how much you can stick to *noticing* things as opposed to trying to *make something* of them. Again, you're not trying to form an opinion. When you enter that rehearsal room, you want to be an informed citizen with an open mind. Stay with gathering material about the play as a whole for as long as you can stand it.

Putting the Character in Context

When you're ready to move on, look over your notes and spend some time taking stock. I think of it as taking the jumble of raw material and sorting it into different storage bins. Later on in the process, it will help me to recall things I've lost track of. However, the most important reason to do it now is that it gives you a chance to figure out how your character functions within the play.

STORY: Imagine that you want to convince a busy producer to come see your play, and she asks you what it's about. She's interested, but she's only got five minutes to talk to you. How would you sum it up? Can you tell the story accurately in a way that conveys the excitement of the piece? Can you give her a sense of the role you'll be playing and how that character fits into the plot? What do you absolutely have to tell her about, and what can you leave out? What are the high points?

If you've read or seen a lot of plays, you've noticed by now that, in terms of plot, the timing of critical moments tends to follow a certain pattern. Near the beginning, for example, there will be an *inciting incident*, which defines what is at issue in the play. A *conflict* is established over the possession of some central *treasure*—Lear's kingdom, the cherry orchard, a buffalo nickel—which has significance over and above any monetary value that may be attached to it. Soon, usually about one third of the way through, there is a *precipitating crisis*—something happens that raises the stakes and makes the conflict very much worse. Scene by scene, the action increases in intensity. Near the end of the play, it reaches a *climax*, an emotional boiling point. Pay especially close attention to this scene; it is often the only point in the play when the major characters are able to say directly what is on their minds. It is literally the play's moment of truth. The very end of the play is the *resolution*, the summing up, the last word, the final image burned onto the retina. What is the playwright leaving us with?

If you can describe these moments—and you can do it with some pitchman's fervor—you have the gist of the story. This will serve you in at least two ways. First, actors are often their own best publicists; when people (and not just busy producers) ask you what you're working on, it helps to be able to rattle off a short, exciting summary. More importantly, as an actor preparing for rehearsals, you're making sure that you know what's important in the story and that you are *invested* in telling it.

YOUR PART IN TELLING THE STORY: Part of being invested in the story is knowing *whose play* it is. Is it your character's? If it isn't, how does your character function in bringing out the story of the main character? What needs special emphasis? If you can answer these questions, when it comes time to do your part as an actor in telling the story, you'll have written your own job description.

For example, say you are playing the religious con man, the title role in Moliere's *Tartuffe*. Despite the title, it's pretty clear that the play is really about Orgon. As a father whose children are of marriageable age, Orgon's frantic embrace of religious asceticism is his way of compensating for a loss of control over his household. It's important to remember that a scene with Orgon is the crux of the play, not just one more con in a series of cons, and that your tactics in winning him over are meant to showcase not just your rascality but his desperation. Bad guys like Tartuffe are not just fascinating on their own terms; they are functional in terms of telling the good guy's story.

THEMES: Okay, remember English class? Themes are not just things you extract from literature in order to generate term papers; they are the bones of the play, the structural elements without which it will not stand. Look over your notes. What events or actions happen more than once in the play? What images, words, ideas recur? What patterns do you notice? Make a list. Like poems, plays are extremely condensed. A good play doesn't contain a single superfluous word or action. If the playwright has used stage time to repeat something, it's important.

You cannot have a play without repetition. *Stories* are built on it—as are jokes: setup, variation, punch line. *Characters* define themselves by going after something repeatedly and with increasing intensity. Repetition makes ordinary objects and words into *symbols* and *metaphors* (maybe the first cigar is just a cigar, but after two or three cigars we begin to wonder). *Ideas*: if a playwright really wants to plant a concept or message in our minds, she will find ways to express it not only forcefully, but repeatedly and in many different guises. Take note.

And while you're listing, pay attention to where the patterns you've noticed shift, break, or reverse. While repetition gets the audience's attention, what sustains that attention is *variation*. And if a theme and its variations go on long enough, we're going to expect a fulfillment, a culmination, a reversal, a *payoff*. Like an orchestra rehearsing a complex piece of music, you, the director, and the rest of the cast will work together to figure out how to play themes and variations so that they have their maximum payoff for the audience.

PLAYING THEMES: Where does your character introduce a pattern or perform a variation? Most importantly, where will you need to deliver the goods, the payoff? For example, in Act V of *A Midsummer Night's Dream*, Bottom's role in the ridiculous play-within-the-play is a send-up of the tragic lover. It's a standout scene and tremendous fun to play. But it gains in resonance if the actor playing Bottom recognizes that he's not just hamming it up; his performance serves as an (unwitting) satire on the behavior of the newlyweds watching him: not just the four young lovers, but Oberon and Titania—and perhaps even Theseus and Hippolyta as well. Their behavior has been no less ridiculous or exaggerated than his own. If he incorporates echoes of their movement or gestures from earlier scenes in the play, it adds further irony and dimension to the scene.

CONFLICTS: Let's re-visit the question of what your play is *about*. Granted, you've already told us what *happens* in the play, and that gives us at least part of the picture. Of course, you're going to want your audience to follow and get hooked on the plot, but is that *all* they are supposed to take away from the experience? What is your opening night audience supposed to take home with them? What might the play *really* be about? One way to address the question is to ask what is at *issue*. Where are the conflicts in the play?

You can start with who's against whom. Characters often have opposites, and when they do, they usually don't just represent him versus her, but *this truth* versus *that*. Plays are about where we as human beings are between a rock and a hard place. We want people to love us, but we can't abide the way loving makes us vulnerable. We believe in telling the truth, and then find ourselves lying in the name of some greater good. We are masters of our fate; we are powerless before destiny.

In the face of these paradoxes, characters go to extremes. They injure each other. They create imbalances that must be corrected and injustices that cry out for redress. Your play doesn't just have a plot; it has an arc, a *trajectory*. For better or worse, the characters are blasted from one place to another. Where do they start? Where do they end? How are they changed? What gets righted? What is resolved by the end? What isn't?

Articulating these conflicts and paradoxes isn't just an intellectual exercise. Again, you are finding ways to invest in the core issues of the play, the tensions that you, the director and the rest of the cast will be trying to make manifest for the audience. In the end, you are not just summing up what is at stake in the play, you are articulating reasons we should *care*.

YOUR CHARACTER'S CONFLICTS: Now, how exactly does your character enter the fray? What part will you have in showing us how we live in paradox? Does your character embody one side of the conflict while another character represents the other side? Does your character remain on only one side or is there a switch? Do the characters find a "third way" in which the conflict is reconciled?

Seek out the conflicts *within* your character. Macbeth, for example, is clearly wracked with doubts and guilt, but he is also ambitious; yes, he is influenced by the three witches' prophecy and by his wife's urgings, but to play him as a man without a will of his own is to shortchange the play. The depth and dimension of your performance in a role will be in direct proportion to the number of seemingly irreconcilable realities you can identify, develop, and sustain. So what strikes you as strange about the character? Again, notice and preserve the weird.

Try summing up your character's *arc*. How does he seem to us in the beginning? If he changes, how is he different at the end? What causes that transformation? When does it occur? The Hamlet who returns from his sea voyage is a different man from the one we meet at the beginning of the play. What happened? You may not know the answer, but at least you can pose the question to yourself before you start rehearsing.

Characters also travel in terms of the audience's favor. We may approve of them in the beginning and not at the end. We may come to appreciate an overlooked character. We may grow to dislike the character who initially charms us. These transitions also factor in the arc of the character. So notice and underscore your initial judgments and feelings about the character, particularly the negative ones. Your audience may react the same way, and it may be important that they do so. The effectiveness of the play may depend, for example, on them disliking you when you first enter and liking you by the end. Your negative judgments are also indicators of where, once you begin rehearsals, you will have work to do as an actor. It's relatively easy to identify with someone you like; the fun begins when you need to identify with someone you *don't* like.

MESSAGE: Every play has something of value to give us. It doesn't have to deal with pressing social or political issues. There need not be a moral to the story or a prescription for what ails us. Even the lightest, most escapist entertainment *means* something to us. It's worth asking not only what's fun and exciting about your play but what's *important* about it.

Bear in mind that what is most important is often unspoken. Theatre's most powerful messages are multi-sensory and metaphorical: Becket's two tramps and a tree, Oedipus blinded, Lady Macbeth sleepwalking. These moments are not important in and of themselves but in what they *represent*. They show us ourselves as we are; they show us what we could be. They are what we dream, what we fear. We're all trying to figure out how to live our lives. What does your play have to offer? What does your character have to offer?

HUMOR AND IRONY: Most often, what a play has to offer us is, on some level, *funny*—funny not just in the sense of what makes us laugh, but also in what strikes us as peculiar or ironic. Through irony, the playwright makes us understand one thing by showing or telling us its opposite. Oedipus claims to see more clearly than anyone else, but it becomes increasingly clear to everyone that he is blind. Irony is a powerful tool because, though we may understand what is told to us directly, we respond much more strongly to what we come to *realize*. Jokes work in much the same way; the comic gives us just enough so we "get it."

Humor and irony are inter-related and inextricable. Frequently realizing one is the key to accessing the other. For example, in rehearsing Chekhov, it's easy to see why the characters' actions (and *in*actions) are ironic, but it can take three weeks of rehearsal for a cast to see why they are funny—and thus to understand why on earth Chekhov insists the play is a comedy. Conversely, in working on a play that is clearly, immediately funny, it can take a while for actors to stop clowning and start doing the serious business of the play, i.e., giving us the irony. Once they start playing up the ironic contrast between the hilarious absurdity of the situation and how seriously the characters take things, they begin to serve both the play and the audience better. If you play it straight—play for irony instead of laughs—you'll get more laughs.

Along the same lines, if you can find what might be darkly funny in a tragedy, you are preparing yourself not just to evoke pity and terror in the audience but also *awareness* that the characters' suffering has a larger meaning. A Lear who can laugh, however bitterly, at his own situation may evoke a stronger sense of irony and a deeper sadness in us. By standing outside his own tragedy for a moment, he increases our understanding.

So before you plunge into rehearsals, set your sights on remembering what is funny and what is ironic about your character. When your performance helps the audience to see what is funny about your character, you are helping us to realize not just the play's humor but also its message. And when you manifest for us the ironies of your character, your audience will not only laugh more often; we will be moved more deeply.

Okay, *now* you can highlight your lines.

Researching the Role

Up to now, you've been working on getting to know the play and developing a guiding vision for your work in rehearsals. As I hope I've made clear, doing this work is foundational; it gives you a solid base to build on. And though others may not see the work itself, they will see the results. Now, as the start of rehearsals draws nearer, it becomes more urgent to make sure you have taken care of some more obvious practical matters.

THE PHYSICAL DEMANDS OF THE ROLE: Start by assessing your training with respect to the particular physical requirements of the play. Does the script mention that your character has any particular skill? For example, do you need to chop vegetables like a chef? Do you perform a sleight-of-hand trick? Will you need to move like a former ballet dancer? I'm going to assume that if you will be required to tap dance, juggle six balls, or perform a Rachmaninoff piano concerto, you already know how or you wouldn't have been cast. It is possible, however, that this show is the first time you'll be fencing or speaking in verse. Get thee to a class. Do research, get coaching. Even if you know you'll be well coached during the rehearsal period, why wait?

Portraying any physical condition or characteristic can take a huge amount of practice. We've all seen actors do unconvincing portrayals of old age, drunkenness, insanity; instead of creating a detailed physicality, they resort to a kind of generalized signaling of the condition in question. Perhaps it's just sloppiness, but even a diligent actor who hasn't had enough time to do research and get coaching can fall into this trap.

If the playwright says the character goes mad, don't just run around the stage twitching and yelling—or go all faux "Ophelia" on us (you know, the glassy wide eyes, the faraway voice). Research the specific mental disorder. If there's no particular disease mentioned, talk to a psychiatrist and figure out a few possibilities. If the character is, for example, schizophrenic, you'd better find out what the range of symptoms of the disease are, what they look like, and what it's like to experience them. Talk to people who are in treatment for schizophrenia. What's it like being on various kinds of meds? The same goes for playing someone with a physical illness or disability. Look it up. Get help.

(Note: You may find that the disease itself is fictional, but even then it's important to figure out the symptoms and play specific effects rather than generalities. If your character turns into a wolf every twenty-eight days, how *exactly* does that happen? As long as you're consistent, you can make it up out of whole cloth. Alternatively, you may want to create a composite out of real-life symptoms: a little something from post-traumatic stress, a little rabies, a tidbit from Tourette's, etc.)

And be aware that once you get into rehearsal, having created a character's impairments, your job is going to be to play *against* them. Someone in pain is trying to overcome it. The stutterer wants to speak fluently. The drunk wants to keep her balance, not lose it. All the more reason to make the condition second nature now.

If the character you are playing is very much older than you are, before you get all wobbly and slow and squeaky-voiced, best pause to consider the range of ways people age. We've all seen the generic octogenarian; prepare yourself to do something different. It's possible your character feels and behaves no differently from someone thirty years younger. It's also possible for her to have a whole range of physical conditions and ailments—and there is no way you will be able to portray this state accurately unless you do research and get coaching on each individual limitation. You shouldn't get attached to anything—when you get into rehearsal, you and the director may decide that the character displays few signs of aging—but it will be easier if you've got a few things to draw on. Get a sense of how people pay attention to a conversation when they're a bit hard of hearing. Work out how you'd move with osteoporosis. Have a little arthritis saved up.

If you're going to be doing an accent, don't wait for rehearsals, start working on it now. There are audiotapes and CDs available for actors to study. Better yet, get a coach if you can—someone who really knows about phonetics. If you can, find a native of the region and tape him saying your lines. Any recordings you can find of native speakers are helpful, as it's not just the sound of the accent you're after, but the music, the shape of it. Also, be aware that regional accents can change substantially in different eras. I've often heard an actor in a contemporary play do a New York accent that hasn't been heard on the street since 1940.

I've listed some physical conditions commonly demanded of actors (and commonly played badly), but there are plenty of uncommon ones. Think carefully about the demands of the role. Don't bluff. Do your homework.

POLICE FILE: While you were reading and re-reading the play, you were trying to get a *feel* for things. As you prepare for the start of rehearsals, you need a good working knowledge of the plain facts of the play. Everything else you've gathered, you've got to be ready and willing to alter, adjust, or simply toss. So what do you *really* know about the character? What does the playwright say about her? What do other characters say about her? What does she say about herself? Usually, the playwright's testimony is the most reliable, but unreliable testimony is evidence, too.

Create a dossier. Try taking a rational, "just the facts, ma'am" approach. Like a cop, you can speculate based on evidence in the script, but don't invent anything wholesale, and don't get attached to your speculations. These are *given*, not invented, circumstances.

QUESTIONS: When I do an inventory of the given circumstances, it usually provides me at least as many questions as answers. You've summed up what you *know* about the character. What can be even more important is what you *want to know*. Even if you think you have a pretty good idea about the character, it's a good idea to review your notes and pull out your questions, especially the ones that really nag you. You want to develop lines of inquiry that will serve you in exploring the character once you get into rehearsals. Lines of inquiry get you in motion. Again, you may need to jettison any answers you've arrived at. Answers are stopping places. Questions are launching pads.

Researching the Play

Your world is not the world of the play. Every place, every time, every social group, every family is distinct from every other. Even if you are working on a play set in your own time and your own country, it still pays to do research. If you are doing a play set before your own adulthood, or the characters belong to a culture other than your own, you're trying to pass yourself off as a native of a world that is alien to you. You've taken care of most of what needs to be done before rehearsals start, but there's still a lot to do.

THE WORLD OF THE PLAY: The research you do should give you a feel for the play's setting, period, and culture; it should get you closer to a sense of being there. If the world of the play is contemporary, direct experience can be a useful teacher. If the characters do something you've never done (and it's not harmful to you or others) try it. If it's a real place, go there if you can. If it's not too long ago, find people who were there and talk to them. Find someone who is a part of the culture (and by culture, I mean *any* discrete social group: cops, New York socialites, Orthodox Jews, etc.); see if he will let you shadow him for a while.

Likewise, when you do library research, try to create for yourself the most direct experience possible. If you are doing a period play, rather than concentrating on "objective" history—you can usually get enough of that from an encyclopedia article—see if you can find first-person accounts—*subjective* history. Be a magpie. Gather bright, shiny things: you want sensations from the time, details of daily life. Good historical fiction can also be useful—if the writer's done her homework, then she may have done some of *yours* for you.

Note: Bear in mind that every character, every situation, every location in a play is *fictional.* Shakespeare's Richard III and Brecht's Galileo may be based on real people, but the historical record may do more to mislead than guide you in playing them. Similarly, Saroyan's San Francisco, Mamet's Chicago, Shakespeare's Athens relate to actual places, but for our purposes, they are chiefly metaphorical. What is significant about these people and places lies in what the *playwright* is using them to *represent*. Don't let your research overwhelm the reality of the play.

THE PLAYWRIGHT: Meet your maker. Read his other work. What ideas or questions does he return to? Who is this person? What does he believe in? What are his politics? What was happening in his life when he wrote the play? If he's living, see if he's done any interviews. If there's a biography, read it.

What kind of mind came up with this play? Unless the playwright is actually a close friend of yours, you can't know for sure, but that's not important; speculate, guess, feed your imagination. Your job is to do him proud, so try to get a sense of what he's like—even if he's been dead for 400 years.

Especially if you are working with a play from another age or culture, you need to get a feel for the playwright's professional world, his theatre. This is the theatre that *formed* the play you are working on, and even if your production does not adopt wholesale all the conventions of the playwright's time and place, they can *inform* your choices. For example, once you take into account that Shakespeare's plays were performed outdoors, in the middle of the afternoon, with little scenery, you begin to grasp just how important his imagery was—and can still be—in creating a theatrical illusion. Just because your production has stage lighting and elaborate scenery doesn't mean you shouldn't use the words to *conjure*. Another example: a lot of actors have trouble sorting out the balance between the extreme emotional situations in Brecht's plays and his insistence that the actor keep her distance from the character's emotions. If you take into account that Brecht's theoretical stance is at least partly the result of his trying to distance himself from the sloppy sentimentalism of the German theatre of his youth—and that the actors he directed in his plays were by no means unemotional—it gives you a little more room to feel as well as think.

PRODUCTION HISTORY: Even if the play is relatively new, you may be able to learn a great deal by finding out different ways directors have staged it, how actors have approached the main roles, and how critics have responded. You can get a sense of the play's (and your particular role's) challenges—and what traps to avoid. For example, if you read that critics of the original production found an actor's performance unrelentingly shrill, you've got a heads-up that the part might be a challenge to structure and modulate. If you're doing a complex play with a long history, it's good to know what interpretations of the play and your role have become traditions. Why not develop your interpretation not just in dialogue with your director but also with your forebears?

If there's a production of the play that is up and running, or a video, think carefully about whether you want to see it or not. Some actors should probably avoid seeing others performing the roles they are about to play. It's possible to fall into a rut of imitation or to become so intimidated by another's performance that an actor becomes paralyzed. But if you know you're not prone to such pitfalls, I say check it out. You may find good things to steal. Better, you may walk away thinking you maybe have one or two *better* ideas. . . .

An Actor Over-Prepares . . .

You've educated yourself about the play and the role. You're well prepared. Now stop.

There are some things you'd probably better hold off on. For example, unless the rehearsal period is extraordinarily short, most actors wait to start memorizing lines until the beginning of blocking rehearsals. By that time, they have a better idea of what the words actually mean and why the character is saying them, and for most actors it's a lot easier to remember words that are associated with movement. (This is not so with learning your vocal part for a musical; by all means, get that under your belt right away.) If you memorize your lines now, you run the risk of implanting your preconceptions of the role along with the words—when an actor does this, it commonly shows up in hard-to-shake vocal patterns.

Save the lion's share of the work for rehearsal. You want to develop your role in collaboration with the director and in relationship with the other actors. Don't actually *work* on the scenes until you work on them in rehearsal. Indeed, until rehearsals are under way, I would recommend you don't even say the lines aloud to yourself—not even once. If you jump the gun by running your scenes with friends—imaginary or real—it's likely you'll start to fix on some interpretation of the role that you'll just have to unlearn. There comes a point where you can't do any more work in isolation. Before you go any further, you *need* the other actors and the director. This isn't just because you want to make sure you don't run afoul of your collaborators. It's because theatre is about what characters do to, with, and for *each other*. When we're in relationship, we strike sparks off one another. So sit tight. It's a light worth waiting for.

CHAPTER 2

At the Table: Use Your Words

IT'S REMARKABLE HOW MUCH EVERYONE—THE CAST, designers, director—gets from hearing the play for the first time. As part of the first day ceremony, the show-and-tell party, you get to see what the designers have been working on, and you get to hear what the director thinks about the play. In return, they get to see you give the role your best guess. Don't cheat them by mumbling out a "neutral" reading. When the actors treat it as a performance, when they speak out and pick up their cues, I'm always surprised by how "finished" this limited first go at a play can sound. I always have the stage manager time it; it's the best measure of how long the actual performance will eventually be. So at the first readthrough, cut loose; act up a storm if you like. Don't worry about getting it right. This is your last chance (at least for a while) to just *play*, so give it a bash.

The next day, it's back to square one. Time to start over and encounter the play again as if for the first time.

Where to Start?

There is a basic logistical problem in early rehearsals. It's awkward having a script in your hands, even more so if you get up and start blocking right away. For reasons already discussed, having the lines memorized in advance is not just difficult to accomplish; it can actually damage the rehearsal process. So most directors spend at least some time sitting at the table so that everyone can get used to the words, get familiar with the basic facts of the dramatic situation, try to figure out what might be under and between the lines, and begin to develop relationships between the characters.

Working at the table isn't a perfect solution, but it has its advantages. First off, if it's done right, there's a camaraderie to sitting around the table with a script, a shared sense of enterprise. Moreover, being at the table gives you an opportunity to concentrate on discovering the power of the play's language without having to worry about what to do with your hands and feet. Sometimes it's easier to recognize the motive force of the voice when the body is relatively still.

But beware: if you're a brainy person, take care that your "table work" doesn't become overly abstract. Keep in mind that this stage of rehearsals is not a preliminary discussion before we begin work, but a plunge into the work itself.

The way to get the most from this relatively sedentary stage is to physicalize it as much as possible. I think the best work at the table happens when actors are aware not only of the physical force of speech and gesture, but also of the constant *possibility* of movement. To this end, I usually have the set already laid out (and if there's a table in the set, use that as the actor's work table). That way, when an actor wants to spontaneously get up and move on the set, she can.

Even at the earliest stages, before you're ready to make larger movements, you can still keep the body involved. One way to think of table work is as if, for some reason, we were not allowed to leave the table and we had to limit our staging to whatever we could accomplish without leaving our places. Every turn of the page, every sip of coffee, every drumming of the fingers can acquire huge significance. It's like when you're driving a car and a good song comes on the radio; in a limited way, you can pretty much get your whole body into it (except maybe your right foot). In rehearsal, instead of crossing towards another actor, you lean forward. You tap your pencil in a moment of impatience; slap the script down on the table. You stand up for a moment and lean over the table, then sit back down. Of course, none of these movements will be part of the eventual blocking, but they keep you from going dead from the neck down. So think of table work as car dancing. Or maybe as acting with one hand tied behind your back: your whole body is engaged; just *wait* till they turn you loose . . .

Then, when it's just about time to start blocking a scene, if your director is game, you can try this:

Exercise: Muse on the Shoulder.

*The principle actors in the scene put down their scripts. Each actor is assigned a muse (the stage manager, his assistant, another actor, etc.) who follows around behind him and gives him all the lines over his shoulder. The prompt should start **while** the other actor is talking. That way, the actor can both pay attention to the other actor and be ready to say his line on cue. The muses shouldn't try to be inconspicuous. In order for the exercise to work, each line should be given loudly and clearly enough that the actor doesn't have to strain to hear it.*

This exercise takes a bit of getting used to. Obviously, there's a technique to the prompting, and, while some actors take to the exercise right away, others may have difficulty listening to both the muse and the other actors. If things are set up properly, the exercise can give everyone great insight into the scene. It can be like a free ride for the actors, as if the script were suddenly and effortlessly implanted in their minds. This is especially true if all the actors have "an ear" for language, that is: if all of you are good aural learners. But if you don't have this kind of memory or ability, it can drive you crazy. I've seen actors make breakthroughs, but I've also seen them quickly reach the point where they're getting ready to swat the prompter as if she were not a muse but a mosquito. If anyone keeps turning around to look at the muse or seems ready to snatch the script out of her hands, it's probably time to move on. . . .

⚊⚊

Trying on the Words

When I'm directing, once we sit down at the table after the initial read-through, first on the agenda is for the actors to just say the words and mean them. All you need to do is try on the words for size. I'm not saying you *shouldn't* act. If you have a strong sense of what to do with a line, there's no point in flattening out your speech. But the pressure's off: no one *has* to act yet. You have permission to go back again and again until a line feels right, or if not right at least *better*. If you stumble or rush through things, I may ask if you want to go back. If you're really having trouble slowing down, I'll ask you to repeat a phrase until it starts to sound better, but I try to keep the emphasis on helping you to slow down rather than badgering you to achieve a particular result.

Exercise: Breathing in the Text.

Let's say we're working on a two-person scene. You and your partner sit as close together as you can and still be physically comfortable—knees to knees is best. You look into each others' eyes. If you've got the first line, you look down at your script and take in as much as you think you'll be able to remember, then you look up at the other actor. Breathe for a moment with the knowledge of the line. Then say the words and mean them. If you forget the words, start again. If the words don't sound right, say them again. If you're in the middle of a sentence and you feel you're off track, start again. Just say the words until they sound somewhat believable to you. You'll know when they feel "right." Saying them probably still feels like faking, but it's the kind of faking you do when you want to fool somebody.

———————

In this early phase of rehearsal, if you are genuinely moved by something, go for it. But if not, I say: opt to keep your voice casual. If a line feels weird, just notice that and keep a straight face. Try the words on as you would a new outfit in a store. Don't buy them yet. Maybe you're not ready. Perhaps the outfit seems a good match right away—it's like other things you already own. Fine. Maybe your first reaction is, "I wouldn't be caught dead in this." Also fine. Eventually, you're going to figure out how to really wear the words, to move in them, to own them instinctively. But for now they feel a little funny, and that's okay. Don't try to sound "natural" by grafting on stutters, "ums," or other tags. Better to live with some discomfort and embarrassment than to shoehorn everything into an extended Jimmy Stewart imitation.

And when the other actor is talking, just look at him and *listen*.

Trying on the words is a brief, but crucial, first stage in text work. Don't try to blast past it, loading everything up with meaning and feeling as if you already knew your character and this is all old hat. Instead spend some time being astonished by everything the characters say and do. Your character chooses *this* word, not that one. Then she does *this*, not that. Hmm.

Note: If you've been reading at a snail's pace for a while, be sure to switch gears. Going slowly for too long can result in a kind of mannered earnestness; details are important, but if every detail remains just as important as every other, things quickly get monotonous. And if the director wants you to take a bolder, more results-oriented approach in rehearsal, that's just fine. Do what she says: pick it up. You can always do your "astonishment" work at home.

Circumstances

EXTERNAL (GIVEN) CIRCUMSTANCES: Of course, the character's words and actions don't stand alone. Your character is saying and doing these things in response to *what's going on* around her. Accordingly, part of the work we do around the table is to nail down whatever facts we can—just as you did when you created a "police file" for your character.

In Stanislavski's *Creating a Role*, the director Tortsov enjoins his actors to distill each scene down to the conditions without which there would be no play. These most basic conditions, what acting teachers call the "given circumstances," are either spelled out or so strongly implied in the text that they're really beyond question. Depending on the director's interpretation, your particular production of the play may have some additional "givens" besides the ones in the script. In a sense, the givens are the ground rules, and the choices we make from here on need to accord with them.

While this process may sound rather detached and unemotional, the *effect* of laying out the givens of a scene is anything but. It's possible for an actor to do the lion's share of the work on the play using this tool alone: "Here's what's going on, so here's what *I do*. . . ." The dramatic situation of the play demands action; it draws us in, gets us pumped up. When you're working on a scene, at some point, be sure to describe your character's circumstances out loud, with feeling. By so doing, you begin to put yourself in the character's place.

But there's a problem: Often, the givens just don't give you enough. Some characters and some dramatic situations are mysterious or ambiguous. Or you may understand a scene intellectually, but still not feel that you "get it." What your character says and does under these external circumstances may not be anything like what *you* would say or do. Even if you could put yourself into exactly the same time, place, culture, and situation in which your character finds herself, you might behave differently. (And if you are playing Medea, I sure *hope* you would behave differently.)

Our actions are not just the result of external conditions but of the circumstances of our *interior* lives—of all that we carry with us including ideas, feelings, memories of past experiences, and so on. The script may imply a good portion of this interior life, but it cannot give you all of it.

At this stage of work around the table, while you and the director are identifying the play's givens, it's useful to notice where the circumstances alone *don't* connect you with your character. At what moment in the scene is it abundantly clear to you that you *aren't* your character? What does the character do that you can't even *imagine* yourself doing? When the circumstances you are given fail you, it's time to experiment with making up a few of your own.

INTERNAL (INVENTED) CIRCUMSTANCES: When I'm directing, I ask a lot of questions at the table. What do you think just happened off stage before your entrance? Why does this character's remark seem to upset your character so much? Why did you marry this person? etc. Usually, I don't want an immediate answer to the question—and sometimes I don't want an answer at all. What I'm doing is establishing lines of inquiry for the actors. I'm asking them to speculate about the things the script doesn't provide. While we're sketching out the given circumstances, I'm trying to help the actor start to color in the rest of the character's external world.

Every open-ended question is a bit of homework. When you're thinking about your character between rehearsals, ask yourself: "What can I add to the story that will clarify, intensify, or personalize the situation for me?" Invented circumstances can be particularly useful when you notice that your character's words or behavior make you uneasy. When you find yourself cringing at the things the playwright is making you do, try making excuses for the character. Every crime has mitigating circumstances; if the play doesn't give you enough, make up some of your own.

For example, let's say you find expressing anger challenging, and you happen to be playing a character who lashes out quite violently against another in the course of a scene. If the script doesn't give you much in the way of justification, you might try imagining in detail some injury that this person has caused your character. Unlike the givens, these added circumstances can shift as needed. As your understanding of the character progresses, you may find that you want to revise or discard your original idea. So be it.

Just how much you should engage in this kind of speculation depends on how it's working for you. You want to make sure that what you're inventing is helping you to carry the role, not just adding excess baggage. Some people find it useful to put together a complete "character biography," but I think it's easy for some actors to go overboard with this kind of exercise. If you suffer from an over-developed sense of responsibility, keep close tabs on yourself. Pay attention to what gives you energy. If, for example, inventing details about your character's long-ago childhood isn't helping you to understand how to play that moment in Act II, Scene 3, forget it; you're just doing busy work.

ANALOGOUS CIRCUMSTANCES: When neither the givens, nor additional invented circumstances seem to be bringing you closer to your character, there's a third type of circumstance that can be extremely effective: the analogy, what Melissa Bruder, et al., in *A Practical Handbook for the Actor*, call the "as-if." Rather than expanding on the play's given circumstances, you imagine a completely *different* set of circumstances, a situation in which you really would behave as your character does. To return to the earlier example, if you can't justify your character's violence toward another, you imagine circumstances under which *you* would become violent. The next time you work on the scene you try it *as if* you were in the situation you have imagined.

Whether they consciously employ this particular technique or not, most directors I know tend to use analogies in working with actors. They say things like "You know your scene with Harry? This time through, treat him *as if* he were an unfriendly pit bull," or, "You know what this situation *reminds* me of . . . ?" Sometimes I'll tell stories from my own life (ones that are unflattering to me seem to be particularly helpful) to help the actor develop analogies.

I don't ask actors to dig around in their own past to look for analogies. Not only are such things none of my business, I'm much more interested in stimulating the actor's imagination than I am in jogging her memory. (More on the uses and abuses of emotion memory later.) In my experience, the most useful analogies for actors are not things they have actually experienced, but things they can *imagine* experiencing. For most of us, life is not as full of drama as it is for our characters. The things we actually do (let us hope) are not as extreme as what we can *imagine* doing.

CONTRADICTORY CIRCUMSTANCES: The given circumstances are the most basic facts of the play and the production, the stuff everyone working on the show needs to agree on. But beyond these basic externals, there is no reason for the actors to agree on what's going on; in fact, agreement can actually be counterproductive.

The reason is that characters often radically disagree about the fundamental nature of what's going on. We've all experienced this phenomenon. You and I are at a party and we witness an argument. Afterwards, I make an offhand remark about what happened, and you're stunned: the two of us don't just disagree about what we saw and heard; my version of events is *so* different from yours that you begin to question whether we were really even in the same room.

Much of a play's conflict (and its irony) can proceed from this kind of contradiction. Indeed, one reason why it's so important for actors not to try to direct each other is that, if one actor tries to bully another into a shared vision of what's happening in a given scene, it can completely undermine the dramatic tension of the material. Remember: you want the other actor not to conform to your vision of the world but to *surprise* you—even if the surprise is unpleasant.

Working with a director, however, actors can collaborate in building *contradictory* perceptions of what's going on, perceptions that intensify both the conflict and the dramatic irony of a scene. Planning out our imagined circumstances and analogies together can become a kind of shared prank: you and the other actor conspire to come into conflict. For example, you decide that he's going to treat the Thanksgiving dinner scene as if it were a sacrament and you'll treat it as if it were a frat party.

Astonishment

I've noticed that actors at the table tend to refer to their characters in the third person; it's only once the show is blocked and the lines memorized that they begin to shift to the first person. In part, this shift is simply the result of the technicalities of blocking; rather than talking about how the character might move, the actor says, "So I get up and cross to him a line later." But I think sometimes there's good reason to hold off identifying with the character for a while. While you certainly want to find connections with your own life, temperament and experience, it can be even more useful to notice the disparities. You are not the character, and unless you want to forever be playing yourself only, you need to do a certain amount of outside appraisal.

Even as you strive to relate, identify, even *merge* with your role, keep a bit of astonishment simmering on the back burner. It's a way to simultaneously play the character and have a conversation with the audience *about* the character. You play what feels true to you, but you also choose what you think will be effective.

Most times, while we're still at the table, you're sufficiently unfamiliar with your role to still have a sense of wonder. We've all still got lots of questions about the play; that helps. But if I sense (at *any* time in the rehearsal process) that actors are taking their characters words or actions for granted, I might throw in an astonishment exercise or two to liven things up. Two examples (both borrowed from Bertolt Brecht):

Exercise: Narrator.

> *Choose a short scene or a section of a scene. As if you are narrating a story, read both your lines and your stage directions aloud. Before or after each line, you add, "He said . . ." By putting each line in quotation marks, you stand apart from the character, both imitating his speech and evaluating his words. By narrating the physical action*

of the play, you show us how your character takes part. Play the scene with some energy and urgency, as if you and the other actors were radio sportscasters at an important event.

―――⬩――

Exercise: Switch Roles.

Just what it sounds like. You get to stand outside your character. Your lines become your cues.

―――⬩――

Sing Out

During the first couple of times through the scene, it's all right if people speak at a normal conversational volume. However, from now on, sing out. You need to start playing in a voice that is loud and clear enough to be understood by everyone in the rehearsal room (about the time you start blocking, you'd best begin speaking at a volume sufficient to reach the back row of the theatre itself). It's not just that you want to practice being audible; it's that picking up the vocal energy and sharpening your articulation forces you to *use* your words.

This early in rehearsals, it's probably best to hold off from too much speculation on *why* characters are saying and doing things. In my experience, it's hard to get at a character's underlying intentions and motivations until you've spent some time walking around in his shoes and saying his words. For now, let's deal with the character's actions (i.e., *what* he says and does). Later on, we'll talk more about what he's *really* up to (i.e., his intentions) and *why* (i.e., his motivations).

Notice first that stage dialogue is not everyday conversation. In a good play, even the most "natural" speech is meant to convey the acute needs of characters whose whole life is played out before us in the space of two hours. As such, the best dialogue, even when it is not overtly poetic, operates in many of the same ways as verse and other forms of overtly "heightened" or formal speech. Each word a character says is part of a calculated effort, not only to get another character to do or feel something, but also to get a reaction from the audience.

Words are tools; while you're at the table, take the time to examine them carefully, pick them up, and play with them. You'll soon get a feel for what they're used for. As you speak the lines, pay attention not only to how the character's words affect others, but also to how speaking them *changes* you.

ACCENTS: As I've said previously, if your character speaks in an accent, don't put off your dialect work, and don't wait until you can do the dialect well to begin using it in rehearsal. Do it badly until you do it better. As Richard Hornby points out, speech is fundamental to identity: "How I speak is what I am." Putting on the sounds and rhythms of dialect is one of the actor's most powerful transformational tools; it gives us a feeling of *otherness*. Doing an accent doesn't just mean pronouncing some words differently. More often than not, it actually involves placing the voice in a completely different part of your mouth.

For example, at the risk of stereotyping (always a danger in dialect work), speaking with a German accent literally requires a stiff upper lip, whereas a Texas accent is so hard in the R's, it almost makes you grind your teeth. Most American accents locate at the back of the mouth and are relatively slurry when it comes to consonants, whereas, Received British, being at the front of the mouth, is the very model of precision. If the majority of a play's characters speak in a particular dialect, I'll often conduct the entire rehearsal period in that dialect. (A caution: sometimes, trying to get the sound of a line right can interfere with your ability to get the sense. If you suspect the accent's getting in the way of solving a problem, drop it for while.) If stage management is game, they get to speak it too. Some of the more gung-ho actors may even extend this "total immersion" to their home life. If you're going to try *that*, best get your family's permission. Don't just show up at breakfast some random Tuesday sounding like Colonel Klink, okay?

Homework: Heightened Language

To some degree, as you are working at the table, just by repeating the words as you rehearse, the sounds, images, and ideas will start to affect you without conscious effort on your part. However, you'll get more out of the language if you support your rehearsal work by spending some time analyzing and exploring the transformative power of your lines at home.

This is especially true of working on a play in verse, but I believe it pays to treat *all* stage dialogue as poetic language. (By the way, don't let anyone tell you that if you can just get the sense of the line across the verse will take care of itself; if you haven't had formal training, you can turn to a number of excellent books—Cicely Berry's *The Actor and The Text* comes to mind—and learn about the specific demands of the form.) Many of the general principles of speaking verse and other types of formal language can apply just as well to more ordinary-seeming forms of dialogue. Some examples:

RHYTHM: Critics have speculated that the reason iambic pentameter works so well is that, in English, it reflects the rhythm of everyday speech. (By contrast, the jog-trot eight-syllable line often shows up in plays as incantation—as in Puck's "If we spirits have offended/Think but this and all is mended"—or as doggerel.) In other words, it doesn't superimpose a rhythm on our speech; rather it amplifies a rhythmical quality that is *already present.*

The whole play—and every part of the play—is in some way rhythmic. Events may move at a steady pace, then accelerate. Objects or people may appear or reappear at regular intervals. Most of all, each character has an inner rhythm, which manifests in her speech and actions. By the mere facts of the pulse, the breath, the act of walking we establish a cadence. Then the heart skips, the breath catches, the runner stumbles, and a new music has taken hold of us.

What rhythms can you find in your character's words and where does the music change? Does she start off with short bursts of single syllables—halting, irregular, staccato—and then gain flow and momentum? Does he pour out volumes of weighty, polysyllabic sound, silencing all the other characters, until he himself is silenced? Does your character's rhythm differ from that of the other characters in the play? Is she going against the flow—or is she the only one flowing?

Exercise: Exaggerated Rhythms.

> As you look over your script at home, read your lines aloud and where you find a rhythm, enlarge it, play with it, mess around. See what it does to your breathing. Get up and move; walk to it; gesture to it; dance to it. It's silly, granted, but sometimes one of the best ways to approach even the most serious material is to exaggerate it to the point of parody.
>
> If you stick with the exercise for a while, you'll notice that some of the exaggerations will give you ideas about or images of the character—both literal and metaphorical—that might merit further exploration in rehearsal. Playing up the rhythm of the line might turn you into a barking dog, a busted accordion or a spreading pool of molasses. You might even find that some of the exaggerations aren't so over the top after all. People—even the ones who aren't barking mad—can be pretty bizarre.

Note: The reason this and the following exercises are for home rather than rehearsal is not that they're weird but rather that they are so minutely detailed and internally focused—you're paying a lot of attention to your own voice and breath. When you get back into rehearsal, you need to focus on communicating with the other actors, not trying to reproduce your rhythmical/vocal experiments. Put your cadence work in the background, like music playing in the next room—though you're not giving it your full attention, you'll notice it still affects you.

VOWELS AND CONSONANTS: I once read about a study, which attempted to gauge the effect of vocalization on the emotional state of the speaker. First, the subject-volunteers were given a test intended to measure their general sense of well being or discomfort. Then, one group was asked to repeat the word "cheese" over and over for a specified period of time; the second was given the word "few." When the volunteers were re-tested, the Cheese group was measurably happier than the Few. Try it yourself. There's a reason we don't ask people to say "few" before we take their picture. I would also argue that, whatever you think of his politics, some of the difficulties Newt Gingrich has encountered in his career are because of his name—it is impossible to say it without screwing up your face as you would in reaction to a bad smell.

You don't have to be an expert in phonetics to notice that the mere physical act of saying a word can affect you emotionally. In everyday life, the sounds of words may not be consonant with their meanings. You may love Newt Gingrich and despise cheese, but in linguistic terms, you're maintaining these preferences *despite* the sound of the words.

On stage, however, more often than not, the sense and sound of words go hand in hand. In part, this is a function of onomatopoeia. When we say "bang" and "crash," we aren't just describing a collision, we are re-enacting it vocally. When we say "stutter," we stutter. Likewise, when we say Bob Dole's name, we aren't just referring to a somewhat dour former senator and presidential candidate with a dark sense of humor; we are mimicking the somber tolling of bells. (Calling him "Robert" only increases the effect.) The mournful effect of the onomatopoeia is further enhanced by possible associations with being doleful or "on the dole." On stage, "Bob Dole" would probably be the name of the creepy funeral director; only in a farce would he end up as the pitchman for Viagra.

But the sound of a word need not recall external phenomena such as tolling bells or babbling brooks (both onomatopoeic expressions, by the way) in order to have an emotional effect on the speaker. The word "disgust" is not onomatopoeic, per se. However, in a slight but significant way, the very act of saying it makes us behave as though we were disgusted. Consider the vowels: "ih" "uh"—not the sounds you make when you are attracted to something. The consonants are just as bad; if you exaggerate them a bit, you'll find yourself, by turns spitting, hissing, and perhaps even (if you place the G back far enough in your gullet) clearing your throat. By contrast, in the course of saying "delight," the vowels first make you smile, then open wide ("ee-eye-ee!"). In terms of consonants, the journey from D to T has the same start and end points, but what a difference that long, sensual L makes.

So as you go over your lines at home, be on the lookout for words in which the sound supports or intensifies the sense. Whether you ultimately choose to play up the effects you discover or to soft-pedal them, it's good to know the range of what the language is offering you.

Exercise: All Breath.

*Try your lines with the consonants minimized or left out. Exaggerate the vowels, particularly where you find assonance (the same vowel repeated within a word or phrase). Again, silly, I know. It works best if you can imagine it as a form of singing, rather than as the result of a severe speech defect. As in the **Exaggerated Rhythm** exercise, when you isolate and exaggerate the vowels in this manner, you can make some surprising discoveries. Here's Helena from* A Midsummer Night's Dream:

What worser place can I beg in your love . . .
Than to be u'sed as you use your dog?

The second line has four "oo" sounds: exaggerate them enough and you'll find yourself howling like a dog.

—⏿⏿—

Though I'm using verse to illustrate, there's no reason why you shouldn't try this with prose. One caution: if you're working on prose, be more selective about the lines you subject to this treatment; if you do it with every single utterance, it will become tiresome pretty fast. I'd suggest working with lines where you've already noticed assonance or lines that occur at particularly emotional moments for the character.

Exercise: Stage Whispers.

Now try your lines in a stage whisper. Minimize the vowels and exaggerate the consonants, particularly where you find alliteration (the same consonant vowel repeated within a word or phrase). Notice what's happening to your face—then notice how the changes in your facial expression affect the rest of your body and your emotions.

For example, in stage whispering Doctor Faustus' line, "Sweet Helen, make me immortal with a kiss," the early W and all the M's that follow make you actually pucker up—as if in anticipation of the kiss at the end of the line!

—⏿⏿—

Again, see how far the exercise can take you, even to the point of parody. Add movement if it helps. Once you've gone over the top with the "kissy-face" quality of Faustus' line, you'll be better able to make subtle use of it later. No one needs to know that, at home, you were channeling Pepe LePew. The same cautions apply as in the previous exercises. Let your discoveries at home inform, not overwhelm, your work in rehearsal. Use the exercise selectively, especially when you're working with prose. Stay with it a while, but if you aren't discovering anything worthwhile, shift to something else.

Exercise: Chakras.

A lot of vocal training is based on the idea that sound comes from the whole body, not just the diaphragm, lungs, larynx, etc. Whether or not this is literally true, it's a useful idea. The sensations that are part of the experience of emotion are often concentrated in a particular part of the body. We might feel fear in the pit of the stomach, for example, or embarrassment in the cheeks. Accordingly, we often refer to emotion, and emotional speech as a localized phenomenon. Off the top of my head, for example: in order to get something off my chest, I may speak from the heart.

For this exercise, think of the body as a complex vocal instrument, a multiple resonator if you will. As each part of the body has a different biological function, it also has a distinct energy. Yoga philosophy identifies seven energy centers (chakras) located midline in the body from the crown of the head to the pelvis. Each chakra is associated with a particular vocal sound. Using your voice to resonate these chakras can help you achieve certain emotional effects in yourself and in your listener:

1. *The crown of the head: "Ng" as in "Sing."*
2. *The mouth/nose: "Mmn" as in "Mmn, tasty!"*
3. *The throat: "Ee" as in "Me."*
4. *The chest: "A" as in "Hey!"*
5. *The navel: "Ah" as in "Ha-ha."*
6. *Just below the belly: "Ooh" as in "You."*
7. *The pelvis: "Oh" as in "Yo!"*

As you explore the resonance of your words at home, you may come across a line that features one of these sounds. In particular, if it's an *assonant word or phrase, or one that seems to bear some emotional weight, you may find that the emotional content of the words is revealed or enhanced by imagining you are speaking **from** the corresponding area of the body.*

—◦◦◦◦—

For example: Stanley in *A Streetcar Named Desire* is a man of appetites, so it's no accident that when he cries out for Stella, the final vowel drawn out to the end of the breath testifies to his hunger: "*Stell*-lahhhhh!" Later, he humiliates Blanche with a forced belly laugh "I say—Ha!—Ha! *Do you hear me?* Ha—ha—ha!" as if he is purging his stomach of the lies she's been feeding him.

Another example: when you say "Oh!" because you forgot to bring your shopping list to the store, the impulse typically comes from the head—you might even precede the exclamation by slapping yourself upside the head. But the "Oh" sounds in Lear's "Blow, winds, and crack your cheeks! Rage, blow!" come from a depth of rage and grief that reaches all the way down and through the core of the body. Along the same lines, you could have the beginning of Romeo's "O, she doth teach the torches to burn bright!" come from the heart: after all, this is love at first sight. But you might want to at least *try* having it come from the pelvis. . . .

Note: Just because you've experimented with a "full-out" vocalization of a sound doesn't mean that you need to do it that way forever after. Sometimes the most effective choice with a "deep" sound is to stifle it and let the audience guess at what has been suppressed. A whisper can be louder than a scream.

Again, it's best to mess around with this kind of exercise mostly at home, but you can also "tune in" to these energy centers before rehearsals and performances by doing vocal warmups that feature "chakra sounds." I sometimes have my actors play chakra-ball, hurling the various sounds at each other as if they were different-sized balls rocketing from the corresponding energy centers. "Yo!" as a bump from the pelvis. "Hey you!" as a fancy double chest/gut move, etc.

IMAGERY, SENSUALITY, AND SYNESTHESIA: Now is your chance to find the sense in your lines, not just in terms of meaning but also of *sensation*. Language, especially poetic language, performs magic for us every day; we transmute the sound of the words into a whole world of sensation. It's not just that we paint pictures with words. Words have taste, smell, and texture. They can give us the feeling of hurtling through space. The technical term for this conversion is synesthesia, but for the actor, it is a kind of alchemy.

Start with the obvious: if the playwright has given you imagery, see it, evoke it, fix it in your mind's eye. Does your character use words to describe sensory experiences—how things look, smell, taste, etc.? When she tells a story about listening to music on a tenement roof on a summer night, do you know what song and what the air smelled like?

But beyond these situations in which a character is *describing* sensations, does the mere sound of the lines *create* other kinds of sensations in you? It's worth noticing, because sensation is closely tied to both motion and emotion.

For example, saying a line may make you "see red," and before you know it, you're pounding your fist on the table; only then do you realize that you're angry. The same applies to the "blue" notes in your lines. Who knows for certain why the color blue, or for that matter a minor chord, should be so commonly associated with sadness, but they are. Often, the synesthesia corresponds to common figures of speech. However, you need not be bound by figures of speech or common associations; if the sound of your words is green, that doesn't mean you're envious. If *this red* makes you feel sad, and *this blue* scares the heck out of you, so be it.

Exercise: Synesthesia.

Read your lines aloud and notice where the sound of your words suggests other kinds of sensation. No need to get stuck in why the words seem this way to you. Just engage your senses. Are your words sweet?

See what happens if you amplify the sweetness. Are they spicy? Acidic? Are they rough? Cold? Sticky? Juicy? Do they grate on you? Are you a smooth talker?

These aren't just figures of speech; they are opportunities to conjure, to transmute sound into something palpable. Take it a step further. What if the words you spoke were objects? What would they be? Some words are caresses; some are stilettos; some are stone walls.

—⚙—

When words take on this kind of physical reality, they acquire both substance and velocity. We speak of the five senses, but we really ought to include a sixth: kinesthesia; that is, the sense of motion through space. It's just as important for our purposes as the other five, and perhaps more so. If saying a line gives you a feeling of movement, use can use that sensation as the basis for action, both in the sense of stage movement and of pursuing the character's wants.

This is not a rational process; it's faster than logic, less reliable, more volatile. Accordingly, it's a good way to open up possibilities and generate raw material. Don't worry if you come up with a good deal of dross; you can use your rational mind to pick out the good stuff later.

Note: When I'm working on a surreal or "absurdist" play, I'll sometimes incorporate this kind of exercise into the process of rehearsing a scene. When the material you are working on doesn't seem to refer to any identifiable workaday reality, the sound and rhythm of the language may be the best entry into the world of the play.

MAKING YOUR POINTS: Stage language, even when it does not at first appear so, is often rhetorically complex. A relatively inarticulate character, even a character of limited vocabulary or intelligence, may encounter a situation in which the need to sway, reach, or persuade others becomes so powerful that individual lines and even extended passages attain a formal structure.

The most obvious examples come in solo passages—not just soliloquies, but also those times when the power of your character's need to speak silences the other characters on stage. However, you shouldn't be surprised to find some sneaky formal constructions in shorter passages, too. In general, if a line contains a complex or compound sentence, i.e., a sentence containing two or more clauses, the character is using a rhetorical construction to make a point.

In order to make sure that you *are* making your point, you need to give some thought to punctuation, word emphasis, and sentence structure. Like complex machines, compound sentences are designed to operate in a certain manner, and it's your job to learn how to drive them properly.

PUNCTUATION: Start with the rules of the road. A comma is not a period. Not only does it have a different function, it *feels* different, just as going over a speed bump feels different from encountering a stone wall. Here's one way to help yourself pay better attention:

Exercise: Punctuation Walk.

> *Sometime the best way to get a feel for the structure of a sentence is to physicalize its punctuation. When you are analyzing a complex sentence, try walking on the words and stopping or changing direction each time you hit a punctuation mark.*

EMPHASIS: The meaning of a sentence can be radically altered by emphasizing one word over another, that is, choosing a key or *primary operative word.* Consider: "I am going to the store." If you hit, say, the second word (I **am** going to the store), it transforms a simple errand to a task you *will* accomplish whatever the odds. If you hit the fifth word (I am going to **the** store), it sounds as if you're headed for shopper's nirvana.

STRUCTURE: A complex sentence doesn't usually give you quite this much free play. Take, for example: "I am going to the store; Frieda is going to the bank." Note the sentence's parallel structure. Do the punctuation walk and you'll find yourself doing a single about face. The point of the line probably has something to do with contrasting the speaker's intended destination and Frieda's: *store* versus *bank*. Both words are important, but which should you choose for primary emphasis?

Stage dialogue is almost always contrived to operate in much the same manner as stage action: it rises. Unlike everyday conversation, each sentence builds to a climax. While there may be important words along the way, like way stations on a railway journey, the sentence's *destination*—and its primary operative word—is almost always at or near the very *end*. When you honor the rising action in your lines, and you avoid the anti-climax of "down endings," your acting is both more audible and more forceful. While there are any number of ways you could say the sentence, if it's a piece of stage dialogue, the odds are you'll be better off with: "*I* am going to the *store; Frieda* is going to the **bank**."

(Note: there are many ways to emphasize a word: you can say it louder, pause slightly before or after it, change the pitch, etc. Most of us have a pretty good innate sense of how to push one word harder than the next. The same applies to creating a rising action within a line: it's not that each word in a sentence needs to be progressively louder than the last; indeed, as long as the *energy* of your delivery increases, the volume can stay the same, or even decrease.)

Of course, to a large extent, as the meaning of a character's line is dictated by her circumstances, so is your choice of primary operative. However, sometimes playing around with word emphasis can help to clarify your understanding of those circumstances. It can even provide you with new perspective on the character's situation.

SINGING SOLO: Once you have figured out how to navigate your character's complex sentences, it's time to do the same with her longer passages. If your character is the only one speaking, the playwright has handed off the ball to you; it is best to formulate a plan of attack before you go charging down the field. The process is analogous to working on complex sentences: to start, you formulate for yourself the character's main point, which will almost inevitably be most directly expressed at or near the end of the speech, then figure out how she gets there. Where are the changes, the way stations along the route? Marking these changes (and perhaps giving the sections a title) will not only help you to realize their full rhetorical force as you work at the table, it will also serve you in the subsequent phases of blocking and memorization. When it comes time to make the journey, you'll have made yourself a map.

For example, here's a passage from Shaw's *Saint Joan*:

Joan: . . . Yes: I am alone on earth: I have always been alone. My father told my brothers to drown me if I would not stay to mind his sheep while France was bleeding to death: France might perish if only our lambs were safe. I thought France would have friends at the court of the king of France; and I find only wolves fighting for pieces of her poor torn body. I thought God would have friends everywhere, because He is the friend of everyone; and in my innocence I believed that you who now cast me out would be like strong towers to keep harm from me. But I am wiser now; and nobody is any the worse for being wiser. [/]Do not think you can frighten me by telling me that I am alone. France is alone; and God is alone; and what is my loneliness before the loneliness of my country and my God? I see now that the loneliness of God is His strength: what would He be if He listened to your jealous little counsels? [/]Well, my loneliness shall be my strength too; it is better to be alone with God; His friendship will not fail me, nor His counsel, nor His love. In His strength I will dare, and dare, and dare, until I die. I will go out now to the common people, and let the love in their eyes comfort me for the hate in yours. You will all be glad to see me burnt; but if I go through the fire I shall go through it to their hearts for ever and ever. And so, God be with me!

Departure: as discussed, Joan's speech, starts as a reaction to a threat: her supposed allies warn that they will abandon her if she continues to fight. Starting from that moment of painful rejection and disappointment, she in turn rejects her allies. *Destination:* By the time Joan says, "God be with me," it is clear to her that no one in the court will bless her, and so she will have to stand alone with God and bless *herself.* Not only is the line a summation of the whole speech, it's an exit line, so you'll need to build up a good head of steam by the end of your trip. *Way stations:* I've inserted slash marks in the monologue where I believe the changes are. First section: She begins by describing her former naiveté and concludes that she is wiser now. Second section: She embraces her current isolation as a mark of Godliness, and so repudiates their counsel on the highest moral grounds. Third section: She resolves to pursue her crusade to her own death and beyond. Note the structure: past, present, *future.*

From Text to Subtext

Back to rehearsal. We've been focusing on what the characters say, but what about what they think but *don't* say? What's going on under the text? What's happening between the lines? Similarly, we've been working on how the characters' external world shapes their behavior, but what about the characters' internal world? The script tells us what the characters say and do, but (soliloquies to the audience aside) it doesn't say what's going on inside them.

Where to start? It's a complex task, so let's break it down. As I've said, I find it helpful to think of the character's inner life as having levels, like the concentric strata of the earth. The surface level consists of the thoughts, emotions, sensations, wants, and memories that the character is *conscious* of in the moment. Descending to the next level, we encounter the character's *pre-consciousness*, the thoughts and feelings, etc., that he is not aware of in the moment, but *could* be. Some of these pre-conscious stimuli, like objects at the limit of his peripheral vision, he might *become* aware of at any moment. Others, though still accessible, are more deeply buried; in order to bring them to consciousness, the character would need the time and inclination to reflect. At the deepest level, we unearth things of which the character is truly *unconscious.*

You may already have ideas, feelings, and judgments about what's happening on the deeper levels. Write them down; they will very likely prove useful later. For now, though, let's concentrate on what's on the surface: the thoughts, wants, and emotions the character is likely to be *aware* of.

UNSPOKEN THOUGHTS: There are some moments on stage that are clearly about thinking. In one scene, a character receives some surprising news, and we "see the gears turning" as she tries to re-orient herself. In another, long after the audience has realized something, we see it dawn on one of the characters. In another, a character starts to say something, then thinks better of it and breaks off in mid-sentence.

We say only a fraction of what we think. Our exchanges with one another are teeming with ellipses and non sequiturs, so much so that written transcripts of everyday conversation are often incoherent—to understand, you literally had to be there. Sometimes stage dialogue replicates and exaggerates this disjointed quality, and sometimes it does the opposite. In Pinter's early plays, the words float on the surface like flotsam from a sunken ship; we only have hints of the catastrophe and the wreckage below. By contrast, Shakespeare's characters will often turn to us and tell us exactly what they *aren't* saying to each other.

No matter what the age or style of the play you are working on, as you try on the words, there will be places where your line doesn't immediately follow from what was said before. Even if your line isn't exactly a non sequitur, you have a feeling that there must be, quite literally, something happening between the lines. In other places, your line breaks off, or is interrupted, before the thought is completed. Sometimes this happens mid-sentence, but not always: some thoughts just seem to overflow the boundaries of the sentences allotted to express them. Some words ring hollow. Perhaps the characters are trading social niceties, and you get the sense that something is going on beneath. And then there are those places where the script indicates that there is a pause, or somehow it just seems right to take a pause.

What's going on? These ellipses, these gaps in the words, these hollowed out places under the words, are all invitations from the playwright to the actor: once you start bridging the gaps, filling the hollows, with unsaid thoughts, you've begun to collaborate in bringing inner life to a character.

Exercise: Bridging the Gaps.

What are the characters thinking but not saying? When I'm directing, I often find it useful to spend some time running a scene with an eye towards tracking the characters' thought processes. Any time you find yourself unable to fill in or bridge a gap, you stop the action and we go back a few lines and give you another run at it. I may also ask you to go back if I feel something's missing, but I try not to push it. This isn't about realizing the director's interpretation; it's about the actors figuring out how to put one thought after another.

*Of course, it's not possible for us to **only** think; our thoughts are interspersed and bound up with feelings, images, sensations, and all the other stimuli rocketing around the nervous system. In practical terms it's virtually impossible to separate cognition from sensation from emotion. For the purpose of this exercise, though, the focus is on thinking. You may not be able to articulate the thoughts or other internal cues that bridge the gap. Again, it's more important to go for the feeling that you have connected one moment to the next. Once you've created a bridge, you'll know it; then you can move on.*

Although the scene isn't blocked yet, it's good to run this exercise with some kind of movement involved, even if it's just crossing to and from the worktable. For some of us, it's hard to think and keep still at the same time.

———

Important: When I do this exercise in rehearsal, the actors don't discuss the scene; they just keep running it. I don't ask them what thoughts they're filling in. In fact, I don't let them tell me. The point is for the actors to realize what feels fake and where the gaps are. Where in the scene do bridges still need to be built? We also don't discuss the circumstances of the scene, the motivations or relationship of the characters.

This exercise is particularly useful when a scene seems to have especially wide or frequent gaps in the logic of the lines. When this is the case, I'll have the actors concentrate on one very small section of the dialogue at a time, maybe a third of a page.

The other place it works well is in exploring the play's transitions. Most of the time, for convenience's sake in rehearsal, the director will break the play up into coherent units or beats—that is, we work from the beginning to the completion of an event, action, or mood. But sometimes it's best to work the transitions themselves, to work from middle to middle rather than from beginning to end. A transition, even if it is not marked by a pause, often means a change in circumstances. Before the characters react to such a change, presumably they need to perceive it, comprehend it, and consider what to do next. Even if the gap ends up being a fraction of a second in performance, at this point in rehearsal it helps to slow it down so that the actors can actually make the transition.

Exercise: Stop and Go.

> The actors do the scene. When I touch your arm, you stop speaking but remain in the scene, thinking about what to say next. When I touch your arm again, you resume speaking the lines as written. Sometimes I'll only stop the actors at places I think they've been rushing or missing something, but other times, I find it useful to stop them at random points, as if the words are failing them.

Warning: unless it's set up properly, this exercise can devolve into a power game. Everyone has to understand that it's not about the director's authority to tell the actors to speak or shut up. Each "stop" needs to be justi-fied as if the actor is running out of words or self-censoring; each "go" should be as if the actor has at last found the words or the courage to plunge ahead.

SURFACE EMOTIONS: Thoughts, emotions, sensations, and physical actions are interwoven and inextricable. Pull on any one thread and you affect all the others. As you speak the character's words and carry out his physical actions, you are bound to be affected emotionally by the process.

When I'm acting, I've noticed that it is useful early on in the process to notice which lines provoke a strong emotional response in me right away. Though these surface emotions may not be the ones I'll feel once I've worked on the role for a while, they serve as immediate contact points. They are a way in, a door not only into the broader realm of the character's emotional life, but also to his wants and the actions he uses to fulfill them. At this point, it may be that what you are feeling will serve as a useful precursor to action. Some emotions *motivate*.

In particular, I've learned to look for places in the script where I feel angry or sad. To me, these are particularly active emotions. They are easily aroused; I feel them as jolts of electricity along my spine and at the base of my skull. The blood rushes to my cheeks, and I feel I must *do something*. Anger, outrage, the feeling that things *must not remain as they are*, can be a call to arms. Sadness can be a hunger, a *crying need I have to fill* right now.

There's no need to limit your attention to anger or sadness. Any emo-tion can be a basis for action. For example, you may find that, when you read, what's on the surface for you is fear. In that case, you may want to explore just how the character needs to fight (i.e., to protect himself) or to flee (i.e., to get the hell out of there).

Of course, in life, emotion can also be a precursor for *inaction*. Our basic animal response to fear can lead us to fight or flee, but it can also lead us to freeze. Similarly, anybody who's ever suffered from depression can tell you how sadness can drain every ounce of energy from your body. However, for obvious reasons, stage characters tend not to be frozen and sapped of ener-gy. They do stuff. In part, that's why we've come to watch them. So, if your character is outwardly listless or apathetic much of the time, you want to be careful about setting off on a course that will land you in a swamp of inertia. Instead, look for the outbursts, the moments when the character bursts the bonds, blows his cool. (Chekhov's characters are a case in point. If the actors playing the three sisters just moon around because no one can get up the *energy* to go to Moscow, we're in for a long evening.) Build your interpretation on the exceptional energetic moments rather than the general torpid impression. Think of the inertia as the lid your character has clamped down on the boiling stew of what's going on below.

Of course, in these first attempts to empathize, it may be painfully clear to you that you are *not* feeling anything close to what the script indicates the character is feeling. Crying is a case in point. What do you do if the script says your character dissolves in tears and all you feel is mild annoyance? Well, good to notice the differences as well as the similarities—at least you know where you are. For now, it's probably better to stick with what you are actually feeling rather than push yourself into a three-hanky sob fest. You're not there yet, so okay: now you know that part of your work is going to be figuring out how to *get* there. Further, the slight anger that you're actually experiencing may turn out to be your best gateway to the character's grief. But more on this later.

For now, just be a good citizen. If the other guy's line is, "Please stop crying. I can't bear it," give at least the indication that you are crying—or will be at some point down the line. Notice what you are actually feeling and use it in the scene rather than trying to suppress it. And at home, as you are thinking about the scene, spend some time trying to articulate what your character seems to *want* at that weepy moment. If you can figure out what she is trying to do, what need she is trying to fill, what task she is trying to accomplish, you'll at least have a sense of purpose in your playing. And, who knows, the emotion you are seeking may just come to you.

SURFACE WANTS: Start with the obvious. At any given point in the play, what is your character trying to physically accomplish? (Bruder, et al. call this part the character's "literal action.") Is she engaged in a task such as washing the dishes, say, or fixing a transmission? Is she trying to get another character to pay her back the money he owes her?

A character's physical, conscious, immediate wants are often readily apparent. He tells us or shows us by his actions. This is what the character *thinks* he wants. If a scene doesn't offer you any clear physical task—if the character seems to be "just talking"—then it's a good idea to name the want that is *just under* the words and give it a physical dimension. For example, if it seems pretty clear to you that a scene involves your character cheering someone up, *get him to smile.* Or, if you figure that your character is attempting to humiliate someone, try to *make him cringe.*

Of course, there is often a big difference between what we think we want and what we *really* want. In a seduction scene, the character may want sex, but what he really desires may be power. And underneath that, he may long for security. Below the character's wants are his desires, and yet further down are his longings.

But we'll get back to those deeper cravings later. Especially at this stage, when you're stuck at the table, it's good to stay with your character's most obvious literal wants. If your character is trying to buy a hot dog and he's rude to the vendor, you may ultimately decide that the transaction is really about his unfulfilled hunger for self-respect. But too much analysis too early can get you stuck in your head. For now, just get the goddamn hotdog.

Listening (and Not Listening)

Often, directors and teachers of acting give notes about listening. They say, "You're not listening to each other," or, "Listen more, just listen." It sounds simple, but it's not. Every time a teacher told me I needed to listen more, although I always had the feeling that the criticism was valid, I had no idea what to do with the direction. So I'd strain away, listening hard, and become tremendously earnest in my performance.

The fact is, in real life, people often *don't* listen terribly well. Little bits of what the other person is saying might be getting through, but for the most part, we're thinking about a host of other things. The same is true of dramatic characters; indeed sometimes, a scene hinges on the characters *not listening* to each other. Beginning actors often ask me, "What do I do when the other person is talking?" I love this question. What I *don't* tell them is, "Listen." Instead, I tell them, "Think about what you want from the other person and what you're going to do or say next. Be like a boxer; look for an opening."

Sometimes even trained actors can be misled by the seeming orderliness of dialogue laid out on the printed page: I say *this*, then you say *that*, and so on, in the sedate rhythm of an amateur tennis match. My character lobs a line over the net and then your character hits it back, and so on. But human interaction isn't a tennis match; if it were, there'd certainly be more than one ball. We'd serve them up whether it was our turn or not; we'd hit some of them back; we'd let some go by us. Sometimes the ball would be heavy as a cannonball, sometimes insubstantial as a soap bubble. Sometimes we'd start hitting balls off into the other courts and completely ignore our opponent.

I've come to realize that the "listening" my teachers were talking about is not a function of earnestly hearing everything the other guy has to say, to the point where you could repeat it back verbatim if there were a quiz. It's about trying to figure out *what's going on* with that other person. We make judgments all the time about what others are thinking, feeling, and especially about what they are trying to do to us, do for us, do with us, do in spite of us. For actors, the skill of "listening" is the ability to tune into a whole range of verbal and nonverbal signals.

For all your work on building an inner life for your character, the best possible way to get to *know* him is to pay attention to, react to, *jam with* what the other actor is giving you. When you speak your character's words, how does the other guy respond? When you try to get something your character wants, how does he receive your efforts? And while we're at it, what does this guy seem to want from you? What does *he* seem to be feeling? Part of your character's inner life consists of trying to figure out what's going on in the *other guy's* head.

In growing up, we discover ourselves not just through introspection but from seeing how others react to us—and so it goes with actors discovering their characters. While you're doing all this internal work, it's good to remind yourself that you're not doing it in isolation. Like a jazz quartet, at its best, the cast of a show is a collaborative ensemble. When one actor tries something, brings a new dynamic to his playing, everyone adjusts accordingly and gets a new feel for his part.

I don't mean to suggest that your character notices *everything* that's going on. Like the rest of us, characters can be exquisitely attuned or utterly deaf and blind to the signals other people are sending. In constructing an inner life for your character, at some point you're going to need to make some decisions about which clues he picks up and which ones he misses. What does he see better than anyone else in the play? More importantly, what is his greatest blind spot? The single most definitive aspect of a character may be what he is incapable of seeing—at least until the final moments of the play. When a play actually brings a character face to face with what he has been blind to, that is, his unconscious life, the revelation can be blinding— as it literally is in *Oedipus Rex*.

But here's the beauty part: you the actor *aren't* blind to it. This means that, in the places where your character is tuned out, you need to be even more tuned in. So while you're at the table, take in all you can, and notice the things your character is incapable of noticing. What opportunities does he pass up? Where does he really blow it? As you work your way downwards through the character's preconscious and unconscious life, you'll be able to make more and more excruciatingly ironic choices. By the time you go on stage, you won't just happen to miss the clues that the audience is picking up, you'll find the most maddening, frustrating, heart-rending ways to ignore them.

Most of the time, if everyone around the table is sufficiently focused, you and the other actors will pick up on and respond to each other's signals. Still, even the best of us get off track from time to time, so here are some exercises that can help you to reconnect:

Exercise: Interrupting.

One way to instantly liven up a scene is for the actors to not wait for their cues but rather to interrupt and speak over each other. For a while, I thought this was just a cheap trick, but then I noticed that the improvement in the actors' performances tended to linger for at least the next few runs of the scene. I've come to believe that shaking up the cues in this manner creates an actual (and sometimes lasting) improvement in the actors' consciousnesses, both of their characters' wants and of the signals they are receiving from each other. By not listening to one another, all of a sudden you begin to listen to each other much better.

Exercise: Back to Back.

Sometimes actors pick up each other's signals better when they can't see one another. I like to do this one with two actors actually sitting back to back so that you can feel the vibration of each other's words. It also works well with the two of you sitting in chairs, not touching, so that you have to rely on pure sound.

Exercise: Incidental Touching.

You find a way to physically touch the other actor at least once per line. Just try it. The inventive ways people find to make contact can give a rehearsal a needed shot of humor; more importantly, you cannot help but make other kinds of contact along with the physical.

Exercise: Echoes.

Start by mimicking or in some way consciously responding to each other's body language at the end of every line. So, say for example that the other guy has the first line and he leans in towards you at the end. You respond by leaning in towards him, then leaning back at the end of your line. Then he leans back, etc.

Once you've established the game in this way, shake it up and make it less mechanical. The next time through the scene, the object is to find as many ways to echo your partner as you can while still remaining true to your own character. If she makes a particular gesture at the beginning of the scene, see if you can use a similar gesture later. If she speaks in a distinctive vocal pattern, pick up on it and give it back to her at some point.

*A third variation is to include negative reflections, to do the **opposite** of what the other character does. He leans forward; you lean back. He sits; you stand. He raises his voice; you whisper. And so on. . . .*

The Line You Hate

As we finish up our work at the table and prepare to start blocking, I usually ask the actors if there are any lines they really despise. (If you're too polite to admit real hatred for a line, I'll settle for simple discomfort.) When you have a line that's just not right, see if you can articulate what's bothering you—and then ask yourself if that is what's *really* bothering you.

Most often, even if your first objection to a line is technical (for example, it's hard to pronounce or it's a cliché), it may turn out that there are other, more complex reasons why the line irritates you. Sometimes, on second thought, you may discover that you actually still don't understand something about the line, or you haven't found a way to fill in the subtext around and under it. Often though, you may find that what you dislike in a line is a great indicator of what you are *resisting about playing the character.*

Remember: language is behavior. Maybe the line *is* a bad line. So what? There's no percentage in playing it half-heartedly. I guarantee you: if you are tepid with this line, other parts of your performance will be tepid as well. If you want to get anywhere with the character, you're going to have to come to terms with this line. In fact, set your sights on making it your *favorite* line. Does saying the line make you feel like a wimp? Well, maybe the character isn't particularly courageous at this moment; what's keeping you from playing that? Does saying the line make you feel underhanded and bitchy? Then stop fighting it and get out your stiletto. Does saying the line make you worry about being impolite? Screw impolite: you've got a job to do.

As an actor, your job is to love your character as completely and wholeheartedly as possible, even *before* you fully understand her—and *especially* if you dislike her. Of course, this applies to relationships in general, not just on stage; as Mariane Williamson points out, if you try to do it the other way around—sit around waiting for your growing understanding to overcome your dislike and inspire love—you've got it backwards. In order to understand people, you have to make the choice to love them first.

Sure, there are things your character says and does that you or the audience may (even should) dislike. But if you allow yourself to believe that any part of your character is unlovable, you will give a limited, distanced, grudging performance. And people may praise you for it, because they, like you, stood outside of the person you were trying to portray and got off on how much better they are. When you accept that your job as an actor is to love a "difficult" character wholly, completely, that's when the real work begins. It means taking the parts of yourself you find unlovable and manifesting them to everyone as worthy of attention and of admiration, not because they are pretty, but because they exist and are a part of you.

This is, of course, embarrassing. But once you take to the stage, it's also not negotiable. The playwright has given you words to use—and use fully. We are all embarrassed about some parts of ourselves. We, the embarrassed, need you to speak for us, and not in a whisper or a guilty mumble. You must sing out.

CHAPTER 3

Blocking: Relationships in Motion

WHETHER YOU'VE HAD THREE WEEKS AT THE TABLE OR THREE DAYS, the beginning of blocking is both a relief and a shock to the system. However physical and dynamic the table work has been, it is liberating to finally really *move*. But getting up from the table with script in hand and trying to figure out where to go, when to sit, when to cross, when to stay still, and so on, can feel like we're all gawky adolescents in our first day of dance class. Further, if all has been going well, we've really gotten into a groove at the table. People have been making discoveries; the scenes have gained both clarity and nuance. Now we're stumbling around trying to figure out where to put our feet.

So here we are. New phase. Start over.

Ultimately (like that awkward teen dance class) this phase of the work is actually about deepening and re-discovering relationships. But before we can really focus on each other, we have to learn the dance steps. We have to solve the basic logistical puzzles of who or what arrives where and when. If the scene involves setting a table, for example, which things do you carry in and in what order do you put them down? Like stage dialogue, stage movement needs to be efficient, helping to set the tone and tell the story with a minimum of wasted movement. We have to make sure that the actors will be seen and heard, that the audience will know where to look, and that the set will be used well.

ORIENTING YOURSELF: Before you start working on a scene, if at all possible, spend some time walking around the rehearsal set, even if it's just tape on the floor and a few chairs. Say, for example, that the scene takes place in a large living room. How might you inhabit this space? Where can you sit, lean, lie down? Are there things to play with, fool with, adjust? What are the reasons you might move to any particular place in the room? What about the placement of objects and furniture will justify a cross left, right, up, or downstage?

Once you've scoped out and tested the places to perch and the ways to get from here to there, get a feel for what you might look at were you actually in such a location. Look for the obvious things that pull people's attention when they aren't gazing at each other. For example, are there windows or is there a fire in the fireplace? A painting? What else might a person stare at when she's searching her mind for the right words to say next? Where might people's eyes drift to when there's an awkward lull in the conversation? If you have time, once you've identified the most prominent "eye magnets" in the set, you might want to throw in a few imaginary details: a pattern on the rug, cracks in the ceiling, a view of the fall foliage, etc.

More importantly, if you're working in proscenium, you're going to want to imagine in some detail what's on or beyond the "fourth wall." Put it this way: so that you may be seen and heard, you as an actor are going to need to justify turning or at least orienting towards the audience. So why would your character turn downstage? Again, is there a window, a view, an approaching iceberg in the distance? Ask your director. If you don't get a clear answer, best make something up.

You should also orient spatially towards the *offstage* places, people, and events your character talks about during the scene. When we talk about things that aren't in front of us, more often than not, we unconsciously gesture in their general direction. If you and I start arguing about Harry after he's gone, even if we don't actually point at the door by which he just left, we will still physically refer to it in some way. The stage left door has become

Harry's proxy and thus the object of my scorn and your protectiveness. By the same token, if something just happened down the street, you need to know in which direction. It's not that you have to draw us a map with your gestures; just knowing is enough to ground you. *Not* knowing may give you the feeling of being lost in space.

Exercise: Walking the Set.

Better than just orienting to the set by yourself, see if you can do it with another actor and take a few minutes to inhabit the room together. Don't run the scene, per se—in fact, you don't even have to speak while you're doing it. Just see what the possibilities are for relating to one another: he sits at the desk, and you stand with your back to him and warm your hands at the fire; he comes to stand beside you; you sit on the sofa, and he goes downstage left to mix a drink; and so on.

Variation: If the scene is any kind of power struggle, it's fun to walk the set as a battle for high status. Treat it like a chess game. He makes a move, you try to top it. He sits behind the desk and puts his feet up; you perch on the corner and knock his feet off. He gets up and walks to the very limit of downstage center facing full out. You follow and stand just behind and to the side of him like a drill sergeant, your face two inches from his ear. . . .

ROUGHING IN THE BLOCKING: As an actor, your job changes at the beginning of blocking rehearsals. Whereas yesterday, you were getting to know your character, today you, the director, and the rest of the cast are engaged in the collective enterprise of working out the basic moves. No matter how well we have prepared, no matter how much information we've gathered, there's no way to create something absolutely faultless on the first go. (Indeed, according to the American Heritage Dictionary, to "block" is to "indicate broadly without great detail; sketch: *block out a plan of action.*") With some blissful exceptions, blocking generally has to be roughed in before it can be refined. We'll go for beautiful, evocative, exciting later—for now, serviceable will do.

Typically, it's not possible (or desirable) for the director to work everything out in advance. Indeed, much of the time, what I've worked out sitting at my desk moving pennies around a ground plan tends to more or less fall apart when I bring it into rehearsal. Most of the directors I know tend to come to blocking rehearsals with a few "must have" pictures in mind, a general sense of what we want the movement to look like from scene to scene, and a plan for entrances and exits. If a scene involves a lot of characters, we'll work out a few more of the moves in advance, if possible. Beyond that, directors depend on actors to figure out where exactly it makes sense to cross, sit, stand, etc. Your help is greatly appreciated.

So how do you act while all this is going on? Some acting coaches advise that you stay in character as much as possible, but I think that's a losing proposition: it's just too hard. My sense is that it will not only be easier, but also more engaging for you if you consciously divide your focus between playing the character and helping to block the play. For now, the nature of the enterprise is technical. This is not to say that you should deadpan your way through scenes and speak in a monotone: play the scenes as fully as you can given all the stops and starts. But rather than expecting yourself to be swept up in the role, remember the work you've done to this point and use all the knowledge and instinct you've acquired to focus on helping the director sketch in the blocking.

How do you help? Obviously, your primary function is to represent your character as a physical presence within the scene. So before rehearsal, revisit the surface wants, the imaginary circumstances, the places where you see shifts or changes occurring. That way, when the director just needs to get you to stage left by a certain point in the scene but doesn't know exactly when the cross should be, you'll probably have a good idea. You may also be able to perceive more quickly when a move runs counter to the character's interests and to suggest alternatives.

You can also be a tremendously helpful player if you keep in mind some general principles of staging. If you haven't had any training in stage deportment, one of the best things you can do is to pick up an old acting textbook. Though, for better or worse, staging tends to be looser these days, the terminology is still in use, so you need to know it. Further, if needed, it helps to know the "proper" way to sit in a chair, for example, or when to use a curved versus a straight cross. Though these "rules" may seem overly formal and restrictive, they are designed to ensure that actors on the proscenium stage will be seen and heard (two of your most fundamental responsibilities), that you can give and take focus at the proper times, and that stage business is accomplished with elegance and economy. It's kind of like table manners; you wouldn't want to use them every day, but far better to know them than not.

OTHER WAYS YOU CAN HELP: These aren't specific to playing your particular character. They're just good practice.

- *Towards, Away, Stay.* Be definite in your movements. If you notice that your feet are wandering, stop. Give yourself three choices in relation to the other actor. You can move towards him, move away from him, or stay put. Choose one. Complete it. Choose another. Everything else is extraneous movement generated solely by an actor's nerves, otherwise known as fidgeting.

- *Give us variety* (or give us death): If you've been fairly leaping about the stage, how about a little stillness? If you've haven't moved for a long time, are you sure you aren't just frozen? If may be that you can find the variety in relationship to another actor: she speeds up and you slow down. Sit-stand, left-right, smooth-sharp, attack-retreat, etc. It's not just a matter of keeping things from getting boring; in order to really see and understand the play, the audience *needs* contrasts. Otherwise, it's as if you're writing with white ink on white paper.

- *Think about the picture.* Every actor I've ever worked with knows instinctively whether the stage picture is engaging or boring. So do you. Keep your peripheral vision engaged. If the picture is flat or unbalanced, see if there's something you can to do liven it up a bit. It doesn't have to be big; sometimes just leaning forward in a chair can help. You can also do wonders for the overall visual quality of the production if you find ways to make use of the *depth* of the stage. There is something thrilling to the eye about seeing actors on different planes—some of them close to us and some far away. It's one of the things theatre is better at than film, so keep your eye out for opportunities.

- *Use the whole stage.* If you've oriented yourself to the set, you know what the possibilities are. If there's a part of the set that no one has visited in a while, see if you can come up with a reason to go there.

- *Don't just cheat out.* When you are talking or listening to another actor, the usual practice in proscenium is to stand on the same plane and turn your body slightly towards the audience. It's a great trick: opens you up, looks natural. But don't let it be the only tool in your kit. In particular, consider if the scene or your character is intense enough that you *must* turn your whole body to the other actor and play the scene in profile. Some people are more directly physically engaged with others, and some are far less. If you think it might work, try playing some moments with your back to the other actor. Try playing a few with your back to the audience. Some actors seem to only project their energy forward, like the headlights of a car. Instead, be a broadcast tower and send your signal out 360 degrees.

- *Move on punctuation.* While you've still got the script in hand, try coordinating your movements with your sentence structure as indicated in the punctuation. For example, if you start a cross away from the other actor at the beginning of a long sentence, stop and turn back towards him on the semicolon; stand still and face him until the comma, then arrive at your armchair by the second comma, and sit (period).

- *Enter in medias res.* Remember the givens, plus the circumstances you invented while you were working at the table. When you enter, be in the midst of physically doing something. You want to give a sense that the character's life continues off stage.

- *Give and take focus.* Who do you think the audience should be looking at? As a rule (with *very* frequent exceptions), look at the person who is supposed to have the focus. Another way: make him the visual exception; if, for example, everyone is standing except for you and him, get up.

- *Justify it later.* When the director is trying to rough in the blocking, it's usually best for things to go like lightning, and you don't want to hold up the process. If she tells you the cross has to come on this particular line, and it feels wrong and weird to you, just do it. You're a smart person; you'll figure out how to make it work later. Plus, remember this is the rough blocking: if the move really is wrong, have some faith that it will get fixed later. Likewise, if you really want to do something, but the director doesn't like it, drop it. Be ready with suggestions, but be just as ready to give them up. Remember: sometimes the director does see things more clearly, and the move you hate now may be the one that helps you come to a new under-standing of the character.

- *Write everything down.* In pencil, please—it's going to change. Yes, writing down the blocking is also the stage manager's job. But she has to get down everybody's blocking. Take responsibility for yours. And the next time the scene is scheduled, go over the moves in advance.

- *Afterwards, memorize.* Once a scene has been blocked, you memorize both your lines and your moves. The next time you work the scene in rehearsal, you want that script out of your hands.

First Runthrough

It's often called a stumble-through, and with good reason. Everybody's self-conscious, people are often still carrying scripts, some of the movement is obviously wrong, and the darned thing takes forever.

In my experience, it is easy for everyone to become lethargic during the stumble-through, and that adds to the problem. The best first runs I've done have been when the cast was clear on the focus and purpose of the task at hand, which is to assess what we've gained, rather than mourn what we've lost, and to orient to the new work ahead. As any parent learns, a developmental leap is often preceded by a regression; sometimes kids forget how to walk just before they run.

In part, the reason we began work at the table rather than on our feet was that, in order to do the right moves for a character, you have to get to know him. The problem is that until you start doing the moves, you can't really know the character. You may want to think of early blocking rehearsals as a kind of crucible in which the work done at the table is tested under high heat and pressure. The good becomes better, and the dross burns away.

TRYING ON THE MOVEMENT: During the stumble-through, try on the blocking in much the same way as you tried on the words during the table work. You don't have to buy it. You don't even have to like it. When you were breathing in the text, your only task was to say the words and mean them. Today, all you need to do is to do the moves definitely. Operate by the "towards, away, stay" rule, and as you do, just notice what's going on inside you.

Probably, as you make each move, the thought that first rises to the surface will have to do with whether it feels right, or awkward, or perhaps just okay. (If your second thought after an awkward move is, "This play is awful," "This director is clueless," or "I suck," try to gently move the thought to the side so you can get on with your work.) This feeling of comfort/discomfort, of excitement/malaise, is good information, but don't stop there; instead, see if you can also notice what's happening in a little more detail—if you can't figure it out in the moment, try thinking it through later—or better yet, walking through it if you can—at home. That way, before you next rehearse each scene, you can solidify what you've gained and come to the stickier moments with a better idea of how to work on them.

What exactly is going on for you? If a scene feels different, how so? Do some of the moves answer lingering questions or help you make transitions you were having trouble with before? Are there places where you feel something is missing, or the blocking seems to be demanding something of you that you can't seem to provide yet? Do some moves feel too big/too small? Are there places where you feel too close to or far from the other actor? Are there places in the scene where you feel embarrassed? Does the blocking give you a different idea about who your character is? Does it run counter to some idea you had about your character? Does it give you new ideas?

Write it down. Be specific. Look over your notes before you rehearse the scene again.

Body Shopping

More homework: if you haven't already started speculating about your character's physical appearance, now is a good time. Whenever you get a chance, make some notes about what you think her face might look like, how tall she is, how she might move or speak. How might her outside be different from your outside? While you probably shouldn't put your ideas into immediate practice, it may be useful to turn them over in your mind throughout the blocking process.

In rehearsal, unless they are explicitly called for in the script, be cautious about experimenting with the funny walk and braying laugh. At this point, as you go shopping for your character's outside, it's important that you don't buy anything. Don't make any decisions now. For most actors, in this phase of the work, the biggest payoff lies in trying to find the character from the inside. So before you start fixing on external "character" choices, wait until you've done some more thorough exploration of the part. Later, as you adjust the blocking and run variations on the scene (see the next chapter), you'll find that some of your ideas fall by the wayside while others stay with you.

Of course, you need to make sure any ideas you have jibe with what the director and costume designer have in mind. Presumably, by now, you've already got an idea of your costume, so you know how the character dresses, and perhaps you know how she wears her hair. Try to find out as much as you can. Is there a plan for your stage makeup? Will you be doing it yourself? If the costume designer and director are open to it, and you have skills with makeup, you might want to start experimenting at home. Olivier once said that, in thinking about creating a character, he always started with the nose.

But beyond contemplating these literal changes to your onstage appearance, spend some time trying to picture the character in your mind's eye. There's no rule that says that, in your own *mind*, you can't be four feet tall, with dark hair, one brown eye and one blue. Actually, you may end up communicating *none* of these choices to the audience in performance. However, over time, thinking of yourself as inhabiting a body of a different size, weight, shape, or color can subtly, or even radically, alter your perception of yourself in relation to others around you, and thus influence your behavior. Some things to try:

- *Profiling*: Ask yourself, "What *kind* of person is this?" For the moment, don't worry about stereotypes or prejudices. Face facts: however enlightened you are, your brain categorizes people, so use the index. If you're playing a bureaucrat, you've already got some ideas of how bureaucrats talk and how they gesture. If you're playing a suburban mom, never mind that every suburban mom looks different from every other, gather your preconceptions—you can challenge them later.

- *Traits:* What qualities does your character project? In general, how would you describe her manner? Is she timid? Warm? Aloof? Stylish? Vivacious? Forceful? Sly? If she were to walk into the rehearsal room, hang out for an hour or two, then leave, what impression would she leave? How would people describe her? If the actors were to do a cheap-shot imitation of her right after she left the room, what would that look like? What's her *signature*?

- *Scanning the street:* How does this character move through the world? How does she sound? Keep your eye out for possibilities when you are in a public place. Does that woman's distinctive walk seem like it might resemble your character's? Try imitating her (don't get caught).

- *Building a composite:* In a sense, maybe you've actually *met* your character before. Think about people you have known with distinctive gestures or mannerisms. Anything familiar or useful there? Ultimately, your physical characterization may be a composite of many different aspects of people you know, read about, see on TV, etc.

- *Animals:* No need to confine yourself to the human realm—one of the best ways to start thinking about the character's physical life is to picture her as an animal. Maybe she's a panther. Or a hummingbird. Or a crustacean.

- *Analogies:* If she were a piece of music, what would it be? What rhythm, tempo, energy do her words suggest? If you needed to use a musical instrument to represent her voice, which would you choose? Or would the sound of your character be not music at all, but some other noise? If she were a painting, which painting? If she were a car, which car? And so on.

- *Self-perception:* What do you think the *character* believes about her own body and voice? How accurate is her self-perception? (Maybe you think she's a crustacean, but does *she* think she's a crustacean?) Does she think she's graceful even though her shins are always a patchwork of bruises? Does she believe that she's disfigured, even though she's gorgeous?

For now, no need to arrive at anything. But invest some time daydreaming. It will pay off later.

From the Outside In

Some actors' process *starts* with this kind of physical characterization. They analyze the play and their role within it, then they create an external image of the character. They experiment with movement, with altering their appearances, their voices. Eventually, they come up with a physical sense of the character that allows them to work on the inner life. This is a valid approach, and if you are blessed with exceptional physical coordination and awareness, you might want to develop your own process to fit this model.

Further, some situations demand this kind of work, so as you develop your skills, you need to gain some facility at working from the outside in. Sometimes you have very limited rehearsal time; you're doing a farce or a musical in summer stock and you need results that read in the back row now. If you're in an audition, and you're doing a cold reading for a "character" role, you need to be able to get in there and make strong choices right away. You may work with a director who demands strong physical choices at the start. You may be involved in rehearsing a piece that doesn't start from a text at all but from physical improvisations. Be ready.

Besides swiftness, the main advantage to an external approach is that actors who use it can often come up with bold, startling results. Further, working from the outside in can circumvent some actors' tendency to intellectualize a role to the point of abstraction—which is a big trap for the actor working from the inside outwards. The disadvantage to the approach is that it often yields glib or hammy results. The actor, having come up with a collection of mannerisms, a funny voice and a limp, thinks he's created a character and stops working. The externals aren't bad but they aren't supported, and the actor is too busy hamming it up to interact with the rest of the cast.

To my mind, it's like building a house by starting with the roof and working your way down to the foundation. But then again, the theatre is a place of miracles, so some people pull it off. If working this way appeals to you, go for it—find the character's mask, his façade—*then* try to find out who is hiding behind it.

Adjustments

If the rough blocking has gone well, the basic pattern of the movement has been laid out. Now that we've tried it on for size, it's time for alterations.

For me this is often the start of the most exciting and rewarding phase of rehearsing a play. As we re-visit each scene over the next week or two, discoveries and breakthroughs tend to come hard and fast. It can also be a frustrating, stressful time for the actor. You're trying hard to get into the scene, but at the same time, you're also trying to get off book and to remember the moves. Still, it is crucial that you bring as much energy, focus, and clarity to the work as possible, especially if you have a short rehearsal period—it may soon be too late for major blocking changes. So you need to do all you can to reduce the static of self-consciousness that often comes with this period of adjustment.

First off, your job will be easier (and your results better) if you begin to approximate in rehearsal as many of the physical realities of performance as possible. Most of us can't rehearse on the actual set until tech week, but a savvy production team will provide you with props and costumes. If a prop hasn't been provided, ask. If you can't get the one you're going to actually use in performance, a rehearsal version will have to do. Having something in your hands is a great way to ground yourself in the physical reality of the moment. Everybody has some degree of free-floating anxiety in rehearsal;

fiddle with a prop—it'll steady your nerves. If you haven't got a prop, Jon Jory suggests keeping a toothpick in your pocket to play with.

The same goes for costumes, especially corsets, fat suits, canes, purses, hats, dresses, shoes, tights, or anything that might affect your movement, posture, or breathing. Actually, I find that it's *always* worthwhile having a rehearsal costume, even if the clothes aren't much different from what I normally wear. Costumes make us feel differently about ourselves, our surroundings, and each other. Changing clothes can be transformative.

The other way you can prepare is to be kind to your body. Eat right. Exercise. Stretch. Bring yourself to rehearsal in good physical condition. (I don't mean you need to have six-pack abs; I'm talking about being relaxed, rested, alert.) Warm up beforehand. You're going to be paying exquisite attention to what your body is telling you.

When you start to play a scene on your feet, you are incorporating (literally, taking into your body) a whole new set of given circumstances. Being in this new space, moving in new ways, you cannot help but feel the effects. There will be times when your movement or your location, in and of itself, will amplify or engender an emotional response in you. The fact that the table and chairs are 20 feet from the couch *changes things*. If, in the scene, your beloved is all the way over there, does it intensify your loneliness? Another example: the last time you played that scene in which the other character tries to seduce you, you just felt irritated by his advances; now that you've been blocked into the downstage left corner, the scene is starting to feel scary.

In other words, before we start thinking about adjusting the blocking, it's good to explore how the blocking *adjusts you*. As with the "line you hate," it may be that the move that feels awkward today is tomorrow's breakthrough. A good director will have insights into your character's psyche or situation that you may not. Sometimes a move that feels bad is just a bad move; but sometimes the move you hate is an indicator of what you are resisting about playing the character.

Keep in mind that some of the moves *should* be a challenge for you to justify. If everything feels comfortable right off, it may be a sign that you're not growing in the part. Make sure that, in seeking to empathize with the character, you aren't minimizing his faults or shrinking him to fit your own personality. Again, in some part of your mind, you want to preserve the weird, the sense of strangeness, of astonishment at how your character moves, talks acts, dresses, behaves. Before you start to make something natural to yourself, it's often better to understand how strange it really is. Otherwise, you're in danger of flattening out the character's idiosyncrasies and cheating the audience of his full humanity.

The new blocking may demand a type or degree of emotion that you hadn't anticipated. Two weeks ago, when you came to the point in the scene where your character asks that crucial question, the other actor was just across the table from you; now, the fact that you need to cross all the way downstage to ask it *makes a difference*. If the cross feels awkward, it might just be a bad or mistimed move. On the other hand, maybe the move is right, and in order to justify it, you're going to have to make the question more important.

Discomfort may also be a sign that you are missing something. Does that moment when you come downstage not feel quite right because it doesn't yet follow naturally from the previous moment? Is there a shift you need to make, a gap you need to fill in order to get from the line to the move? As in the *Bridging the Gaps* exercise in on page 45, this phase of rehearsal often involves running very small sections of text over and over in order to fill in the missing pieces and complete the transitions. Sometimes a textual gap you thought you'd bridged at the table has widened now that you're on the rehearsal set. Or perhaps the blocking has created a new gap. What image, idea, thought would get you from the line to the movement?

Yes, it's intense work, but try to stay loose. Luckily, you don't have to figure this out all by yourself. We're all stumbling, but most often, with each other's support, we lurch *forward*. While you may be the only one playing your character, everybody's trying to figure out what will be best for the moment, the scene, the play. In a good working session, there's a lively exchange between the actors and the director about what works, what doesn't, what's missing, what might be better. When something doesn't feel right, speak up. Articulate the problem if you can. Ask to run that last bit again. If you've got an idea, try it. As you try to decipher all your internal chatter, the emotions, sensations, and thoughts that are ricocheting around your mind and body, and as you try to sort out the useful messages from the noise, remember: when you get stuck, *look to your collaborators for an answer.*

Intentions and Relationships

From this point on, any time you feel you are struggling with a scene, look to the other actor. More often than not, the answer isn't inside you; it's over there. When you lose your way, look over at the other actor and ask yourself:

- *What do I really want from this person?*
- *Who is he to me?*
- *How will I know when I get what I want?*
- *What's in my way?*

At the table, we dealt with the character's surface wants, but now that we are in the blocking phase it's time to go deeper. Up to this point, I've tried to stay away from talking explicitly about your character's underlying intentions. My experience is that, until about the time they're ready to put down the scripts, it can be difficult for actors to articulate their characters' hidden agendas. Work at the table can get so "heady" that I'd much rather have you feel your way along.

But now you've had some time in rehearsal to get to know one another. Now you and these other people are moving around, towards, away from each other. Now you're moving *in relationship*, so let's try to put a name to some of these dances you're doing—especially when the moves don't seem quite right yet. In short, when a scene doesn't seem to be catching fire, try lighting a fire under yourself by stating your character's *intention* with respect to the other character.

An intention is a kind of formula meant to spur you to action, put you in touch with the other actor, and help you to invest emotionally in the outcome. It has four ingredients—most of the time, you'll probably want to stir them into the mix in this order:

- A desire
- A relationship
- An objective
- An obstacle

Let's say, for example, that you're playing a scene from a play set in a small American town in the 1950's in which your character is trying to seduce a guy she's been dating for a while. One day, before you run the scene (which has been kind of flat), the director takes you aside and asks, "What do you want from this guy?" So you start with what's near the surface, just below the words:

I'm coming on to him.

The director says okay, but could you go a little deeper? Why? Is it just sex you want? And you think, well yes and no. Sex would be good, but what I really **desire** is to get married and get out of this town. So you say,

I want him to save me.

That seems right, says the director, but the **relationship** is vague. Does he look like a savior to you? So you look over at the other actor and you think about his character's slowness to act and seeming inability to pick up on all the seductive hints your character is putting out. He's never even kissed you. It's so frustrating. So you say:

I want to seduce this half-wit sonofabitch.

That's better, says the director. Now you've got a relationship. Before, he was just a guy to you. Now he's a half-wit sonofabitch. Keep the insult; I do think you're angry with him on some level. But you switched the **objective**; now it sounds like you're going to do something *to* him. Instead, let's make sure that you're trying to get something *from* him. What do you want to get *him* to do right now? So you say,

I want to get this half-wit sonofabitch to kiss me already.

Great! But before we do the scene, one more thing: So why don't you just kiss him? Why all the hinting? What's the **obstacle**? So you think about the work you've done on what it was like to be a woman in this time and place. You think about how invested your character is in the conventions of middle-class romance and marriage. And she's not getting any younger, so she can't blow this chance. You think about how vicious people can be when a woman is "too forward," or worse, "too easy."

I want this half-wit sonofabitch to kiss me already, but I've got to make it seem like it's his idea. I can't let him think I'm cheap.

You look over at the other actor, repeat your intention a couple of times under your breath. *Now* you're in relationship. Now when you do the scene, you are truly engaged with the other actor, and so you are better able to sort out whether the blocking—and all the choices you make that come along with it—are bringing you closer to what you want from him.

That's the process. Let me explain it in a bit more detail:

DESIRES: Again, they're deeper and by far less rational than simple, surface wants. While the character isn't *unconscious* of these desires, they may be lurking just outside of her peripheral vision—which is another reason to hold off articulating them unless they don't seem to be spontaneously rising up in you. Desire is more fluid and faster than language. We don't drive desire; it drives *us*. Before we know it, it manifests in us on a physical and emotional level, and more often than not, we keep silent about it or lie about it, even as we do all we can to resist or fulfill it. We're simply in the ring with the other person. Often times, we don't even *know* what we want. We get flashes, pictures of what would be good to happen right now, but for the most part we're flying blind.

Surface wants are self-explanatory. She comes on to him because she wants sex. But sometimes when you're playing the surface want, you feel something's missing. The character's behavior isn't straightforward; it's too odd or extreme. Just playing the surface want is not nearly enough to justify the emotional content of the scene. In this case, you get the sense that there's an edge of *desperation* under her flirting. Ironically, you realize, she really isn't all that seductive: she's too clingy. She seems more angry and scared than sexy. So then, what *is* she up to?

In your mind's eye, you scan what you know of the character's life at this moment, looking for what might be making her so desperate: What's making her angry? What's she scared of? You think about all her frustrations with her family and friends. You think about how scared she is of becoming like her mother: tired, dumpy, rigid, conventional. No, it's not really (or not *only*) sex she wants. It's not even really him she wants. She wants *out*. "Then why doesn't she just leave?" you ask yourself. Maybe that's what you would do. It seems only rational to you.

But then you realize she's not rational. The rational mind isn't driving this bus; there's a desire at the wheel. She wants to be *rescued*.

RELATIONSHIPS (AND EPITHETS): But a generalized desire isn't enough. She wants to be rescued by this man in this moment. So who is he to you? Again, he seems an unlikely candidate for "savior," so let's find something to call him. "Boyfriend" is too literal and too generic—as is most any term you might find on an application form: father, wife, friend, co-worker, etc. Relationships change, often radically, from moment to moment. Brothers can be allies one moment and enemies the next. Perhaps the reason she *started* going out with this guy is that he seemed like a plausible rescuer at the time. So given that he's not playing the role your character once assigned him, what does that make him now? Certainly a dreadful disappointment. Still, she hasn't given up on him, so what should you call him?

Epithets work. Both insults and endearments contain sensational emotional content and potential for action. When you affectionately call someone your knight in shining armor, it's not just flattery; it's a whole narrative in miniature. In this case, calling him a *half-wit sonofabitch* can contain all your fears of your life going down the drain. Insulting his intelligence implies that if you could only get him to switch his brain back on, he might respond to your advances—and that if he does not respond, he's just another dumb townie who isn't going to take you anywhere.

Unlike generic descriptions, epithets either express or imply a status difference between you and the other actor. It's more obvious with insults, also known as "put downs," but it's also true of endearments: while calling someone your "baby" or your "cutie-pie" may not actually be intended to diminish that person as such, it emphasizes the part of the romance that is based on his vulnerability, childlike innocence, sweetness, smallness. And where there is a status difference, there is a transaction going on.

I should clarify what I mean by status. It's possible to base an entire system of acting on observing and playing with status differences, as Keith Johnstone does in *Impro*. I'm not necessarily referring to such fixed indicators of status as rank or social position, though they can certainly affect status. Status is fluid, changing from one minute to the next; under the right circumstances, a homeless drunk can intimidate a corporate CEO. People manipulate status all the time. We're quite good at it, and the transactions can be remarkably subtle. Self-deprecating humor is a good example: you attempt to raise your status with respect to someone else by seeming to lower it. Further, people's desire is not always for higher status. Not everyone wants to be at the top of the pecking order. Indeed, in the scene we're discussing, your character would much *prefer* to be low status. Indeed, she may be *playing* low status in order to get her man to *step up* (all the more reason to resent him).

So when you're trying to formulate your character's underlying intention, think about whether you see the other guy as above, below or even with your status level at this moment, then invent a juicy epithet that epitomizes that status relationship. Who is he to you? The love of your life? A mosquito buzzing around your ear? A trusted mentor? A Judas? A shining light? A sleazeball? A reliable partner? A partner in crime? A vicious rottweiler? A cop?

As you think of him, so you will behave towards him.

OBJECTIVES: Now here's where the rubber meets the road. You've got a desire and a relationship, both of which compel you to *do something*. But what makes a scene really pop is when you are compelled to compel *the other guy* to do something. Let's call it a *double compulsion*: "I *have* to *make* him . . ." "I *must* get her to . . ." "I *need* to *persuade* him to . . ." "I'm *going* to *force* him to . . ."

Force him to *what*? Give your intention a physical payoff. Give yourself a goal. Like a fighter in the ring, you're not just throwing punches; you have to make sure they connect. How else will you know whether you are moving towards your desire or away from it? How will you know when you've won? Can you see it in your mind's eye? Can you almost taste it?

Focus on the moment when the tide will turn your way. In the case of the reluctant boyfriend, though the surface want may clearly be sex, given the past history of the relationship, it's probably best to set your sights on his leaning over and, at last, *kissing you*. It's tangible. It's plausible. And if you can just get there, *then* you'll worry about the next step.

OBSTACLES: Most engines have a governor, a device that ensures the machine won't run so fast that it does itself damage. So do we. If desire is our engine, our governor is our ability to imagine the possible adverse consequences—either of failure to achieve what we desire, or of success. In this case, your character is constrained by visions of both failure *and* success. If she fails to get him to express any kind of physical affection, she'll be stuck where she is, which is intolerable. If she is "too forward," that in itself may turn him off. Worse, if she succeeds in seducing him, but leaves him with the impression that she's "too easy," she'll lose both her man and her respectability.

In plays, every desire has an obstacle. Otherwise, there'd be no play. So don't just ask yourself what your character really wants; ask: what's in the way of achieving it now? Achieving it directly, simply? If your character could just kiss the guy, she would. If she could skip town, she would. More than anything else, it's the obstacle that makes the drama. It both suppresses direct expression of the character's desire and increases its importance.

The higher the bar, the more energy it takes to clear it. If you want to raise the stakes, try a bigger obstacle.

BEATS: When the character's circumstances radically change, so does her relationship with the other character—and thus her intention towards him. In the scene, if he gives you a long kiss, then gets down on one knee and proposes marriage, he's probably not a half-wit sonofabitch any more. You may still want to seduce him, but instead of trying to get him to throw you a lifeline, your intention may be more along the lines of sealing the deal. Likewise, if he gives you a long kiss, then reveals that he's just this morning proposed marriage to your sister, your relationship has changed. New circumstances call for a new analysis. What do you want now? Who is he to you *now*? How will you know when you get what you want? What's in your way *now*?

Most often, these major changes (also known as "beats") will force your character to abandon one surface want and replace it with another. If he's proposed to your sister, for example, perhaps the stage directions tell you to shift from attempted seduction to attempted strangulation. That's a pretty good indication that your relationship has changed.

When you are working with the director to adjust the blocking, one of your mutual tasks is to find proper ways to mark and punctuate these transitions. If a shift isn't working properly, try formulating one intention for *before* the change and another one for *after*. Then see how your body wants to move.

SOLILOQUIES: What if you're *alone* on stage? Basically, the same rules apply. The only thing that's different is the *location* of the other guy: he's out in the audience. Sometimes this means that you are actually speaking to the people who have come to see the show tonight, and they've become the other guy. Ask yourself the same questions: What do you want from them? Who are they to you? Are they on your side, or do you think they're likely to judge you harshly? What do you want them to think, to believe? What do you want them to do?

Sometimes your character is talking to herself. Now, I don't know about you, but when I talk to myself, I've got several different personae who may be on the other end of the line on any given day. There's a part of me that's still a small scared child and needs a loving pep talk. There's a bonehead who needs to be slapped silly. There's a higher self who inspires me. So when your character is talking to herself, the first question is: *which* self is it?

Then: what do you want from that self? How will you know when you've got it? What's in your way?

Locate that inner self somewhere out in the audience—and make sure it hears you when you talk. This might feel weird at first, but there's really no alternative. You'll get used to it.

A Few Cautions:

- Don't intellectualize this. Articulating the nature of your character's intentions and relationships can be a powerful tool, particularly if you love and respond to nuance in language. Not everyone does. If you are a kinesthetic actor, don't beat yourself up if you can't find the right phrase. Instead, when you are thinking about your scene at home, try finding a sound and movement that seems to fit or intensify what's going on inside you, then recall it before you go on stage. Much better to articulate the character's desire with a groan and a lunge than to get stuck in semantics.

- *Intention is not the same as motivation.* So far, we've been exploring what your character wants, and then what she *really* wants. We're still not talking about *why* she wants it. The question *why* tends to lead to intellectual, *psychological* answers. Psychologizing your character isn't bad in itself, but save it for later in the process when you are ready to incorporate her *unconscious* longings into your portrayal. Okay, perhaps the reason she's so fixated on this distant, dim boyfriend, rather than finding someone more responsive to love, is that he's like her father. Interesting, but it probably won't help you right now. Write it down. We'll get to it.

- *Take care of business.* Sometimes the physical task at hand is terribly, overpoweringly urgent, like, say, getting someone to put down a weapon. Sometimes it's less so. In any case, before you try out your theories about what your character's underlying motivation might be, be sure to take care of business: remind yourself of anything physical the script calls for your character to accomplish. Just as you need to operate within the given circumstances of the play and the production, you should make sure your interpretation of the character's actions doesn't overwhelm their literal reality.

- *The plan is not the reality.* If you were a general, and this were a battle, you would gather your best intelligence, then formulate a plan of attack. If the enemy's forces turned out to be in a different location or more powerful than you had anticipated, you wouldn't stick to the original plan. As an actor, your intention is the plan. Go over it in your mind. Think about how you might go about pursuing your objectives. Visualize success. Then, as you walk on stage, *forget it*. The other actor is throwing things at you: words, insinuations, body language, furniture. Don't pretend it's not happening; deal with what's hitting you upside the head. Chuck the plan, and respond to the reality.

- *An intention is your little secret.* Most often, a stated intention is something you design and build at home and then test drive in rehearsal. No one but you needs to know what's under the hood. You may be working with a director who speaks the same language and can help you formulate or adjust intentions, but in the end, it's your business. In fact, when I'm engaging an actor in this kind of conversation, I usually do it *sotto voce* on the sidelines. Discussing your intentions with other actors can be counterproductive, particularly if your characters' relationship in a given scene is in any way adversarial. You don't want to compromise your ability to surprise each other.

Refining Your Intentions

Once you've got a workable intention, try tinkering with it a bit. Here are some tools for tuning up:

INTENSIVES: One way to give a quick boost to the energy or immediacy of your intention is to reduce it to a command. Before you start the scene, you look at the other actor, and you mutter under your breath:

Kiss me, you half-wit sonofabitch!

Though I've tried to keep it relatively low-key, you may have noticed that, in formulating a character's underlying intention, the language I'm inclined to use tends towards the obscene and/or the blasphemous. When I'm coaching actors, I'll sometimes urge them to use profanity to get to the bottom of things. I can get along without cussing if I have to, but it does feel a bit like trying to cut a steak with a butter knife. As Hauser and Reich point out, not only is the word "fucking," one of English's most effective intensives ("goddamn" is also useful), it can serve as both adjective and adverb. If you want to raise the urgency of your intention, try employing it liberally:

> *I want this half-wit sonofabitch to fucking kiss me already, but I've got to make it seem like it's his fucking idea. I can't let him think I'm fucking cheap.*

As Charles Marowitz writes, "A rehearsal that doesn't begin in the boiler room will never make it to the penthouse." Sometimes, especially if you tend to be a "nice" person, using profanity can be not just intensive but actually incisive, allowing you to cut through the protective layers of politeness and getting you in touch with what is vulgar, earthy, juicy, about your character's desires.

If it just makes you uncomfortable, forget it; there are other ways. But let us not dismiss out of hand the way of the potty-mouth.

OUTER AND INNER MOVEMENTS: Characters try many times and in many different ways to get what they want. In part, that's why we're interested in them. As you make adjustments and try variations on the basic blocking of the scene, re-examine whether you are crediting your character with enough ingenuity to employ a variety of tactics. This means finding variation not only in your physical but also your psychological maneuvers. As your character's surface wants float on top of a deeper desire, an underlying intention, so, too, each movement, each gesture you make, each line you say on stage has under it an *inner movement*.

I'm sure I don't need to list for you the possible physical tactics in a seduction scene—though it's probably worth saying that in this case, your character may be severely limited in what she feels she can physically express. But thinking through what inner moves might be available is another matter. Obviously, you could start by *dropping a hint, buttering him up, getting under his guard.* Notice that even though these can be subtle inner movements, we talk about them as if they were overtly physical. Even if you don't actually touch him, you can use your words, your eyes, to *stroke, caress, cozy up* to him. Though these tactics are so obvious as to be clichés, you do need them in your bag of tricks. But don't stop there; if, as the scene progresses, your character becomes increasingly frustrated, you might try *needling* him, *shaming* him, *calling* him *out,* even *hitting* him over the head. In desperation, you might *beg, plead, threaten* him. If all else fails, you might even *reason* with him.

Note that, as epithets suggest or create status relationships, each of these tactics is in its own way a status maneuver. Any conflict, negotiation, or interaction can contain hundreds of these little adjustments: you lower yourself, you raise him up, you put him down, and so on.

When we were roughing in the blocking, each time you chose a definite movement or stillness (following the *Towards, Away, Stay* rule), you were manifesting human relationships in their simplest form. On the most basic level, we attract or repel each other; we move one another or we remain unmoved. But even the least intelligent person among us is ingenious at social manipulation. Now that you're refining the rough blocking, see how many maneuvers you can find.

ANALOGIES REVISITED: As I'm sure you've noticed, formulating an underlying intention for your character can lead to a re-evaluation both of the circumstances the play has given you and of those you may have invented to put yourself in the character's shoes. Often, seeing your character's relationships in a new light affects your perspective on the rest of her world. Accordingly, this is a good time to re-think any analogies (or "as-ifs") you may have been working with, and perhaps to come up with new scenarios that better fit your new understanding of what drives your character. The question, as Bruder, et al., phrase it, is, "*What does this situation mean to me?*"

There is no right answer to this question. It's an exercise in imagination. Still, it's worth being precise; do pay attention to the emotional *effect* of your answer. Because different scenarios involve different consequences for failure, your choice can raise or lower the stakes in the scene considerably. It's one thing to play as if your job were at stake, another to play as if your life were at stake, still another to play as if your child's life were at stake.

Indeed, depending on the fantasy you conjure up, it is likely that you will underscore some aspects of your character's situation and soft-pedal others. In this case: one scenario may emphasize the outrageousness of his seeming indifference to your plight and de-emphasize the fear of the consequences of failure. Another may bring to prominence *both* the sense of entitlement to his affection *and* the embarrassment of offering yourself sexually to someone who isn't responding. A third might play up the urgency of your need to escape, and play down the necessity of subterfuge. Off the top of my head, some examples:

- *It is as if you've fallen and hurt your ankle. He comes along and, rather than helping you up, he's just standing there making conversation.*
- *It is as if you were stranded without any money in a bus terminal late at night. You're trying to coax a few dollars out of a stranger.*
- *It is as if your house is on fire. You're locked in. He's an idiot child. He has the key.*
- *It is as if you've put years into being a volunteer at a non-profit organization. Now they've created a new position that exactly matches the work you have been doing. This man has the power to hire you, but he's keeping his options open . . .*
- *It is as if you're already half-naked, and he's too preoccupied to notice.*
- *It is as if, in a town where anti-gay violence is a regular occurrence, you were trying to seduce a woman. You **think** she's a lesbian, but . . .*

When you've got a spare moment, it can't hurt to come up with more than one possibility. That way, when you or the director want to change the emotional tone of the scene, you'll have some quick ways to jump-start your imagination and to re-calibrate what's at stake.

Meanwhile, Back in Rehearsal . . .

As the relationships and intentions get adjusted so does the blocking—and *vice versa*. As we begin to regard one another differently, the dance we're doing changes. Each time we change the dance, we see each other in a new light.

I've spent so much of this chapter describing an internal approach to character precisely because the work you are doing in this phase is so markedly, though hopefully not exclusively, focused on externals. With any luck, by now, the moves you, the director, and the other actors have worked out are having a strong effect on your inner life. Likewise, your internal work manifests in crisp, appropriate and uncluttered stage action. As you move into the next phase of rehearsal, when you look over at the other actor, *pay attention to what moves you*. Literally. Now that you're more in tune with your character's desires and more fully immersed in her relationships, in any given moment your body may be wiser than your brain. Be on the look-out for tensions, twitches, and other slight movements—what poker players call "tells." Sometimes that barely perceptible jerk in your knee means your body wants to take the cross a line earlier. Follow.

CHAPTER 4

Variations: Looking Deeper

BY NOW, THE BLOCKING IS JUST ABOUT FINISHED. Though nothing's set in stone, at least in terms of movement, the play looks pretty much the way it will in performance. Look at any given scene in the play, and you'll find it's just about the best it has ever been. Still, for all that's been accomplished, it feels as if there's a lot further to go. There's a difference between playing at a scene and really *living there*. It's off, somehow, unbalanced. In some scenes, something's missing, but it's hard to be sure what. In others, you may think you know what needs fixing, but somehow the solution seems to be just beyond your grasp. However well the work is going, there is the tantalizing sense of being on the edge of something much more exciting. It's as if we've got a perfectly fine black and white image of the play. What will it take to give it color and dimension?

Where do we go from here?

Time to switch gears once again. Over the past week or two, the focus has been on making fine adjustments, trying to get the blocking right. If we keep on *adjusting* things, trying to finally *nail* that killer scene or that tough speech, we're headed for trouble. As opening night draws ever closer, everyone's feeling under pressure to get the show *right*. But we can't get there from here—at least not by adjusting, correcting, or settling things. We'll "set" the play later. Right now, it's time to shake it up.

These days, rehearsals alternate between running longer sections and working on individual scenes. In the next chapter, I'll talk more about how to think about the longer sections and prepare for runthroughs. For now, let's keep focusing on the smaller units, because that's still where most of the discoveries are likely to happen.

The devil is still in the details. For all our hard work, there are aspects of each scene, and facets of each character, to which we are still as good as blind. It's not that we can't see them, but we haven't thought to look. So what's there just outside of our understanding? What possibilities are hovering in our peripheral vision but haven't yet come into our sights?

The best way that I've found to delve more deeply into the work is to take a deep breath, put aside some of the expectations we've accrued, and do some exploring. We all know what a shallow performance looks like. If the actor is emotionally involved at all with the character, it's only on one emotional level. She sounds the same note over and over. Even if she varies the volume or the tempo, it's the same note. Conversely, a complex, dimensional performance can make us laugh, cry, and shiver with outrage in the space of a few moments. You need to experience and express not just the over-arching emotional tone that the scene *seems* at first glance to require, but also the various other emotional shadings that may run underneath or even counter to it.

How to get there? This is a time when we need, not fewer possibilities, but more. At this point, instead of trying to get a scene one-kind-of-right, it usually makes more sense to get it all-kinds-of-wrong. By distorting the scene, exaggerating one element, neglecting another, grafting on yet another, we gain fresh perspectives, new possibilities.

It's a kind of natural selection—though not nearly as haphazard. Each variation on the scene, each mutation if you will, has something to offer us. You wouldn't want to play the whole thing that way in front of an audience, but in each distorted run of the scene, there's usually a moment (or even a whole section) when the mutation works, when it's better than anything we've done up to now. There's no intent to keep the scenes in these distorted forms. Instead, each time through, the actors learn what possibilities are in the scene that just haven't occurred to them. We keep what suits us and forget the rest.

So here are some variations to try. Each exercise is designed to call to your attention some aspect of your character's emotional life or behavior that you may, on some level, be resisting coming to terms with or have simply overlooked. The sequencing of the variations is deliberate (again, usually it makes sense to work downward from what's on the surface), but really you could start anywhere. I wouldn't suggest trying *all* the variations—I can't imagine you'll have time. Rather, as you're reading through these suggestions, keep in mind a scene you're working on. Then, as you might choose spices off a rack, pick the variations you think most likely to liven things up: let's try a little more of *this* . . .

Emotional Variations

I like to start this phase of rehearsal by playing around with the emotional content of the scene. Where might your character be angry? Sad? Fearful? No doubt, you and I have a few notions about what emotions the character might be feeling (and which she might express), but until now, we haven't really talked that much about emotions. The time hasn't been right.

There's good reason for this mutual reticence. Most experienced directors are reluctant to ask actors for any particular emotion by name. Too often, the consequence of asking an actor to "be sadder" is either contempt or fakery. These days, most actors have been repeatedly admonished not to *try to* feel emotions. Many acting teachers speak of emotion as something that is beyond our control. We can't generate it; we can only approach it obliquely.

They've got a point: in general, if we try to dictate our emotional response to any moment, we're in trouble because we aren't responding to what's actually happening but to a pre-conceived notion. Far better to concentrate on the character's intentions and let the emotions come.

As doctrines go, this admonition to regard emotion not as a goal but as an outcome of pursuing other goals is both valid and practical. Among other benefits, sticking to the character's actions and objectives helps to counteract the push for instant, superficial results.

Mindful of these factors, directors have learned to be cagey, to work with actors in ways that invite or imply, rather than suggesting or prescribing, emotional responses. We emphasize the given circumstances, or use analogies, or tell stories from our own lives. But, however cleverly directors and actors avoid the e-word, the subtext of the conversation between us has everything to do with instigating emotion.

When you as an actor seek to empathize with the character, *by definition* you are pursuing, or at least preparing the ground for, certain emotional states. You are looking for anything that might provoke you to feel as the character feels. Further, you often have ample evidence that the character is feeling a *particular* emotion. If she tries to strangle her boyfriend, she's probably mad, no? Even when the stage directions don't give you such a blatant prompt, you undoubtedly still have ideas, or at least guesses, about what the character might be feeling.

The problem with working directly on a character's emotional life is less a matter of technique than it is of timing. If you "play angry" too early, all you get is a generalized wash of anger. But now that you've created such a wealth of emotionally suggestive internal and external details, why should we continue to keep mum about the character's feelings? You've long since planted the seeds of an emotional life, let's survey the ground and see what's taken root and what, with a little care, might bear fruit.

WHAT TO LOOK FOR: Before we start digging around, let's get an idea of what exactly we're looking for. The experience of emotion is so complex, so entangled with all the other functions of human physiology and psychology that it is difficult to consider in isolation. We feel emotions *both* in the mind and in the body, and whether the physical state of arousal occurs first and triggers the mental state, or vice versa, is a matter of longstanding debate. For our purposes, however, it's a chicken-and-egg question: there is no point in our waking life that is not a continuous round-robin of thoughts, physical sensations, emotions, memories, and other muscular, glandular, and neurochemical events. Each function of the mind and body affects every other function.

Accordingly, it is possible to step in anywhere in the cycle and affect the whole system. In effect, this is what we've been doing all along: all our invented circumstances, artfully constructed relationships, and imaginative analogies are lies we fabricate in order to create a feeling of emotional engagement with a fictional world. By consistently and repeatedly feeding false data into the system, we alter our internal ecology. Supply yourself with enough imagined prompts to anger, and the blood starts to boil.

But if you pay close attention, you'll notice that you're not *just* angry. It's rare that we gripped by a "pure" emotion; most of the time, the mind and body dart from one emotional state to another, to yet another, and back again. Most of the time, we are in a state of mixed—or composite emotions.

BASIC EMOTIONS AND COMPOSITES: According to some neuroscientists, there are five basic emotions, that is to say, emotional experiences that cannot be broken down into smaller emotional units: joy, sadness, anger, fear, and love. Others would add disgust to the list (though it's possible to regard disgust as a composite of anger and fear). There is some dispute as to whether emotional pain (as opposed to purely physical pain) should be on the list; is it a discreet experience, or is it really the same thing as sadness? Shame might also deserve its own niche in the hall of primary emotions, but, if so, it would surely be right next to pain: picture the moment of embarrassment, the stab in the gut, the blood rushing to your cheeks as if you'd just been slapped. . . .

The basic emotions are the colors in our palette, or if you like, the tones in our scale. While the individual elements are fairly limited in number, the possible combinations supply us with a cornucopia of emotional states. Some of these composite emotions are relatively simple: For example, what we call pride is often mostly a simple social variant of joy—though, depending on the situation, there can also be undercurrents of anger (as in, for example, the pride of defeating an enemy) or love (as in the pride of seeing a child take her first steps). Other composites are mind-blowingly complex: jealousy, for example, can be made up of various degrees of anger, love, sadness, pain, fear, shame, and disgust. While the basic emotions tend to be relatively fleeting, some composite emotional states (Stanislavski refers to them as "passions") can go on indefinitely: the word "happiness," for example can be used to describe the feeling of a moment, a day, a year or an entire lifetime—however many painful and contradictory emotions that life may contain.

Some complex states are based more on quashing emotion than experiencing it. The species of discontent we call boredom, for example, usually results from suppressing outright sadness (at not receiving the stimulation we crave) and anger (blaming someone else for it)—and perhaps only letting these pent-up feelings out through a small hole (also known as whining).

Other terms for emotion have less to do with identifying combinations of feelings than with describing variations in intensity. If you had a built-in volume dial for anger, for example, your lowest setting might be mild irritation; turn it up a few notches and you'd be mad, then irate, and so on up to a state of rabid fury. But for now, let's stick with calling the basic emotions by their generic names; there's a clarity and simplicity about recognizing that you're *angry*. If it's better for the scene and the character, you can change it to "miffed" later.

At this point in rehearsals, in exploring the emotional possibilities of a scene, I find the most helpful approach is to keep our attention on the components—the individual dots of color in the pointillist painting, the separate notes in the chord—rather than trying to play everything at once. Like the painter or the musician, we're ultimately going to put it all together, but let's break it down first.

WHERE TO START? Emotions come in layers: you might feel anger on top of sadness on top of fear. Most often, unless we do some exploring, we may be aware of the top layer but not of what lies beneath. So, once again, let's start with the conscious and work our way downward, inward.

Actually, probably what's closest to the surface is not strictly emotion but the simple awareness of pleasure and pain. Starting with what's pleasing, what's fun about doing a scene, can give you pretty good access to what the character might be joyful about. Similarly, even if we don't show it, people tend to be aware of pain, and to have an immediate and at least somewhat conscious emotional reaction to it, most often sadness and/or anger.

Besides being the most directly tied to the pleasure/pain response, joy, anger, and sadness tend to be at the surface of consciousness because they are—at least in the part of the world I'm familiar with—the most socially acceptable to express (though, in general, there are stronger taboos against anger in women and sadness in men).

But even these emotions can be deeply buried. Think about it: which of the basic emotions is completely safe for us to express fully, out loud, in public? Not joy—unless maybe you've just won the lottery or the World Series. A lot of people have trouble expressing more than mild satisfaction. Not anger. Instead, we say we are "a little disappointed." Sadness? Nope. Not in this culture, anyway. Just listen to the euphemisms people trot out around a grieving family when someone dies. Fear? Sorry: As the T-shirt says, "No Fear;" especially not for guys. Love? Maybe the hardest of all. Try even just telling someone outside of your immediate family that you love him. Say it in the blandest way possible; it's still hard for most of us to do. As we learn in junior high, never mind love, even expressing *enthusiasm* can lead to ridicule.

As we repeatedly and ever more expertly hide our emotions, we begin to lose track of them. The same applies to characters in plays. If anything, they face even stronger constraints, and so may repress feelings even more deeply. Again, like us, characters have secrets. Without secrets, no drama.

SCANNING FOR EMOTION. In the course of playing a role, as in the rest of our lives, most of us tend not to have much of a say over *which* emotions we feel. However, when it comes to *how long* an emotion lasts, *how intensely* we allow ourselves to experience it, and *how openly* we express it, we are much more in command. If we start from the assumption that, given all the work you've put into in the scene you are working on, the emotions are *already there*, we should be able to discover and enlarge on them. In the first part of each of the following variations, I ask the actors not to try to create the particular emotion but simply to be on the lookout for it, amplify it as much as possible, and use every opportunity to express it.

If people get a little hammy, that's okay, but it's not really what we're looking for. There's a difference between overdoing and overacting. The object is to take the emotion a little bit "over the top," to bring it out as far as possible without simply faking it. Cranking it up all the way can give you a sense of the limits of the scene—which may lie beyond where you thought they were. Turn it up as far as the scene will bear, and maybe a little more. If you find that you're overacting, take a deep breath, focus on the other actor, and go back to scanning for what's true.

You should also expect that other emotions will come up as well; no need to stifle or play them down. If you're scanning for joy and suddenly feel a rush of anger or sadness, that's a discovery in and of itself. If it's true, turn it up and let it out. Let us see and hear it.

In the second part of the variation, the actors continue to scan for and amplify the emotion internally. This time, however, to object is to *contain* the emotion, to try to hide it from us. If you try to hide it from us and, once or twice in the scene, *fail to hide it* that's even better.

Probably, the second variation is closer to what you'll want to do in performance. If you express too much emotion, we won't feel it. It's not just that some people in your audience shy away from emotional displays. There is a theatrical mechanism at work here. If a playwright tells us everything, he bores us. If he leaves something out, we have to guess; therefore, we become involved in the play. Likewise, if you as an actor only hint at an emotion, we have to fill it in ourselves. The very act of imagining how you feel stirs emotions in us. That's why, with respect to emotion, the actor's *job* is to struggle to overcome it—and fail.

(As a rule, the same goes for humor: if you laugh, we don't have to. That's why so many great comic actors have a "deadpan" style. They know it's funny, but they let us "get it.")

One way to think of these variations is that, in the first part, you play the scene "pedal to the metal," as if—at least as far as the emotion in question is concerned—there were no social constraints whatsoever on you or the character. You make no effort to hide the feeling at all. In effect, there's no subtext anymore. Got a feeling? Blurt it out. In the second part, you keep the accelerator down, but at the same time, you hit the brakes. The emotion is every bit as large, but the social constraints are *enormous*. In the first part, if you cut your finger, you'd scream so loud the neighbors would call 911. In the second part, if someone shot you, before you sank unobtrusively to the floor, you might very well apologize for bleeding on the carpet.

For clarity's sake, I've laid out the variations below systematically, proceeding from what's usually near the surface downward to what's usually covered up. However, in general, I'd suggest starting with the emotion your character is most clearly manifesting in the scene. Once you've played it to the hilt, then covered it up, try another variation. I start here with joy and end with love, but there's no reason why you shouldn't begin, say, with sadness and end with fear.

Sometimes, especially when there are more than three or four actors in a scene, I'll use the technique with only one actor as opposed to having everyone involved. When two or more actors are working on the same variation, there's often a kind of chain-reaction; if both people are scanning for anger, for example, they tend to piss each other off. However, sometimes it's useful to have two actors work contrasting variations simultaneously: he scans for anger while she scans for sadness, for example.

Note: If you're working on a show now, and you're interested in trying the technique, be sure to let your director know what you're up to before you go bending the scene all out of shape. You don't have to go into a lot of detail; just tell her that, in order to find the right level, you're interested in messing around with overplaying and underplaying the scene. You want to try taking a few things over the top then pulling them back. Most directors I know incorporate some version of this over/underplaying phase into their process, so you're likely to have her support. However, if she doesn't want you to overplay, you can always limit yourself to simply scanning for emotional content and making more subtle adjustments based on what you learn.

THE JOY VARIATIONS: What is your character enjoying about this scene? Sometimes the things that give us pleasure are so odd or unexpected that we fail to notice, let alone celebrate them. Before running this variation, remember that joy doesn't have to be *nice*. If schadenfreude (or sadism) is your character's thing, you can have just as much fun as someone who's all hearts, rainbows, and bunny rabbits. Shakespeare's worst villains fairly dance a jig as they plan to eviscerate the good guy. Even if your character is in the middle of a painful crisis, you may be able to find considerable joy there. Each time Shaw's Saint Joan is betrayed, she fairly splits her breeches in her rush to leap to the moral high ground. Don't tell me that isn't fun. Even the worst moment of agony may have some joy in it— if only in the certain knowledge that the worst has finally arrived. It might seem a strange question, but is it possible that, in a way, it is a *relief* for Oedipus to blind himself?

Exercise: Circle of Fears.

If there's nothing fun about the scene lately, I'll sometimes do this as a warmup to the Joy Variations. I set a time limit for the exercise, say, ten minutes. Everyone sits in a circle. You name something you're afraid of. Then the next person says something he's afraid of, and so on, around the circle. Repeats are allowed—i.e., you're allowed to be afraid of the same thing as the next guy—but you shouldn't repeat something you've already mentioned. If you can't think of anything at the moment, you can pass. If everyone in the circle passes, the exercise is over. But that's unlikely; once it gets going the game will probably fill whatever time allotted for it.

The usual result is that people feel lighter, freer, more able to do the joy or love variations. I can't say for sure why this is, but I'm guessing it has something to do with how much effort we typically spend in pretending we aren't afraid. Just saying what we're afraid of can be a kind of relaxation exercise.

*If you aren't relaxed after this exercise, if you're **more** scared than before, you might have more fun working on the darker stuff: maybe the fear variation, but the anger or sadness variations might also yield results.*

———

THE ANGER VARIATIONS: Blame somebody. As you play the scene, any time something is painful or in any way unpleasant, any time something goes wrong, any time you're *afraid* something *might* go wrong, anytime something isn't what you expected, anytime something is *just* what you expected, assign blame. Blame the other character, blame this town, blame the President, blame your boss, blame your parents, blame God. And if any pity, compassion, or sadness comes up, blame yourself for being a sucker, then get back to blaming other people.

Depending on the scene, another way to scan for anger—particularly moral outrage—is to look for what disgusts you. As with pain, disgust can have a purely physical origin; something literally stinks and we turn up our noses. But the reverse can also be true: we find that other guy's behavior (or attitude, appearance, tactlessness, etc.) revolting, and the stomach turns.

Anger is a secondary emotion, arising in reaction to or defense against pain, fear, or sadness. If you get *really* angry, you may find yourself actually incorporating these other emotions *into the anger*. Ever been so exasperated that you found yourself trembling or weeping with rage?

Whether or not you find enough in the scene to take you quite that far, it's worth remembering, as discussed earlier, that anger is great motive force.

Having trouble connecting with your character's intentions today? Ask yourself what the hell's wrong with that other character over there. Then go fix his wagon.

Exercise: You-You.

Try this as a warmup for the anger variations. Draw an imaginary line down the middle of the room; you and another actor stand opposite one another on either side of the line. The only word spoken from the beginning to the end of the exercise is, "You." Neither of you may cross the line or touch the other person. It's a game, and you're both playing to win. If you want to get more actors involved, appoint a judge. After a minute or two, the judge decides a winner, and the loser steps down and is replaced by a new challenger.

Usually, the people who win are the ones who are willing and able to employ a wide arsenal of tactics. They can get loud and in the other guy's face, for example, but they can just as easily stay aloof and make the other guy look bad for losing his cool.

After a couple of rounds of this, run the scene. All the players, even (especially) the losers, will probably find plenty of reasons for their characters to be angry.

Exercise: Bitch.

Run part of the scene. The actors play the scene as written but insert the word "bitch" into every line or tack it on at the end. As in: "I'm home, bitch." "Hi bitch, how was work?" "Bitch, it's a jungle out there." And so on.

Try to play it straight. But even if you laugh all the way through it, you'll find there's an edge both to your voice and your feelings towards the other actor. (Men seem to have a particularly strong reaction to being called bitches.)

Then run the scene without saying bitch, but **thinking** *it the whole time.*

⚬

THE SADNESS VARIATIONS: The way to find sadness is to look for pain. It shouldn't be hard to find; like as not, your character takes quite a bit of punishment over the course of a play. People insult you, elbow you out of the way, ignore you, disappoint you, and so on.

As with the other variations, you may find that when you scan for sadness, other feelings come up more readily or frequently. In particular, a lot of people tend to get mad before they can acknowledge that they're hurt. If you know you're prone to this kind of compensating behavior, when you run the scene, scan for anger, then see if you can find the pain underneath and stay with it. Often, there will be sadness there if you allow it to come up. (If your personal tendency around sadness is towards paralysis, be careful: we're after grief here, not numbness. If you find yourself sinking into lethargy, best try another variation.)

Pay special attention to what the character wants and can't seem to have. *Hunger* is an especially useful link to sadness for the actor; it implies an unfulfilled need, a longing. The longing can be especially intense (involving not just dull pain, but sharp *pangs*) if it is focused on the past, as remorse for things your character wishes she hadn't done, or as nostalgia for something she has lost. But specific causes for remorse or sadness are sometimes beside the point. To paraphrase Elvis Costello, sometimes we have no idea what it is that we want, but that's not the point; the point is that we want it *now*. For most of us who live in relative material abundance, the saddest feeling comes with acknowledging that however much we consume or achieve, there's something missing. We're still starving.

Again, when you are trying to get your bearings in a scene, sadness can be a useful goad to action. It's like when, after an unsatisfying day, you find yourself staring blankly into the open refrigerator: for God's sake, you want *something*. Look at that other character over there; maybe *he's* got something that will satisfy you. Go see.

Exercise: "Ow."

> *Try a run of the scene in which, every time something is hurtful, including every time you try and fail to get what you want, you physicalize the pain and say "Ow." If it's particularly bad, voice it from deeper in your body: say "Oh." Variation: touch the place where it hurts (your head, your gut, your heart, your eyes—or is it a pain in the ass?).*

THE FEAR VARIATIONS: Harriet Walter suggests that one of the best ways to really understand a character is to ask yourself what she fears. Indeed, almost everything your character does may be understood as a reaction to fear.

What is your character worried about? One way to approach scanning for fear in the scene is to keep your eye on the consequences of failure for your character. But that may not be enough. Some fears are so personal, so individual, that analogy and substitution may be the only way you can connect to your character's *particular* anxieties. If you can imagine an analogous set of consequences (an as-if) that scares the bejeebers out of you, you're on your way.

But that may not work, so let's go for a sure thing. One thing both you and your character are guaranteed to be afraid of is *other people*. When people are asked what they fear the most, they mention a host of things, including heights, deep water, dogs, snakes, cars, and bugs. (Interestingly death comes in at only number seven on the hit parade, while financial problems are number four.) What's number one? We are. Speaking in front of a group is the most frequently mentioned phobia. Why should that be? Is it just the number of people—the potential of public shaming? Certainly, that's part of it, but then, in my experience, it's just as possible to scare yourself silly by getting up to speak in front of two people, or even one person, as it is in front of a hundred.

Everyone's frightened of everyone else. How could we not be? There is nothing so potentially dangerous, corrupt, depraved, irresponsible, wild, and vicious as a human being. And yet we depend on these creatures for company, comfort, sustenance. If you just let yourself consider it for a second, that other person doing the scene with you is *terrifying*. Viewed from this perspective, every bit of confidence your character exudes is a smokescreen. Every cocksure aggression is a pre-emptive defense. Every romantic gesture hides a fear of loss. There's a man behind the curtain, and he's scared shitless.

So before you start the scene, take a moment to look over at that other actor. Your character needs something from him. Think about it. Scary, huh?

Exercise: In Your Face.

> As warmup for the fear variations, take a moment to consider how scary people can be. Then you and your scene partner sit, stand, or lie next to each other with your noses just a few inches apart. Get as close as you can without your vision blurring. Gaze into one another's eyes. Stay that way for a few minutes. If that doesn't freak you out enough, try saying "I love you" to each other. No jokes—it has to be sincere.
>
> If you get the giggles, that's okay; it's a pretty good sign you're scared. If you can stand it, let the giggles die down, hang on for a minute more. Then try the scene.

THE LOVE VARIATIONS: One of the cool things about acting is that you get to love strangers.

Maybe I better clarify what I mean by "love," because we use the word to describe a whole lot of very different things. First, the love I'm talking about isn't sexual attraction; though sex can be an expression of love, it can also be an expression of just about anything else. Nor am I talking about romantic love or "falling in love" which, though it may include love, is a complex mélange of different emotions, desires, and needs, not to mention fantasies. I'm not talking about the "deep" love that people associate with successful marriages and other long-term relationships. The love I'm talking about is a simple emotion as evanescent as any other: you have the feeling towards someone for a moment, and the next moment, you're on to something else. You may feel it more frequently towards your sweetie, but you can also feel it towards someone you hardly know.

Not only is it possible to feel love towards a relative stranger, sometimes it's easier. Not knowing the person, having no shared history, we're not encumbered by complexities, ambivalence, grudges, etc. It's not just naiveté; there's a kind of purity to it: we're free to simply love something about them without complication. We have fewer obstacles. We see them as they are: as lovable as the children they once were. Indeed, if you can hold this compassionate perspective, it's possible to love someone you dislike. Of all the compound emotional states, loving someone, in the sense of "falling in love" may be the one we have least control of—I suppose that's why we don't call it "leaping in love." Paradoxically, of the basic emotions, love is the one we most often refer to as an act of will. If you work at it hard enough, you might even be able to love your enemies—and wouldn't *that* be novel.

Since the feeling of love is very close to that of simple enjoyment, you may be able to start scanning for it in the scene just by noticing again where the scene is fun, but this time in a way that emphasizes a positive attachment to others. In particular, where might your character enjoy the other people in the scene? Where might she feel connected with them? Where might she want to make that connection stronger?

It may help to ask yourself what you admire in the other characters. Look at the other actor before you start the scene. Isn't that character he's playing amazing? Even if he's utterly loathsome, don't you love how clever, how complex and sneaky he is?

But if the scene is full of conflict, and this kind of Pollyanna thing isn't for you, you can just stick with looking for the desire to connect. At some level, we really do *want* to love one another. It can happen, astonishingly, in the midst of the most terrible of battles. A midnight moment of silence between barrages, and you realize the soldier in the frozen trench across the field is yelling for you to have a Happy New Year.

Exercise: Incidental Touching Revisited.

*Same rules as described on page 52. You find a way to physically touch the other actor at least once per line. Obviously, it can make the first "Love Variation"—where the object is to amplify and express love wherever you can find it in the scene—easier. But you may also want to run the touching exercise as part of the full-out **Anger** variation; if you do, (besides reminding everyone not to physically hurt one another) add the stipulation that at least one of the touches must be some form of caress. It can make for a nice break in the hostilities—or for a terrible escalation.*

EMOTIONAL PROMPTS: Not everyone can do this scanning thing without help. As I've said, by the time we reach adolescence, most of us have learned the skill of containing emotion so well that we not only lose the ability to express it: we can't even *recognize* it. If asked, we're "fine." Accordingly, before running an emotional variation (unless I'm working with actors who have uncommonly good access to every aspect of their emotional lives), I find it's sometimes useful to use a brief exercise designed to stimulate the basic emotion and remind us all what it feels like. Then, while you're playing the scene, it's easier to scan for, sustain, enlarge, and express the emotion.

Maybe this sounds esoteric, but really it's an everyday phenomenon. Think of it this way: we humans are highly suggestible and apt to project our moods onto whatever, and whoever, happens to be around us. If you're in a "bad mood," every possible irritant becomes more prominent. When I start my day feeling sad, it's not unusual for me to weep at pop songs on the car radio (it's amazing how much we're free to express only in the privacy of automobiles) or even TV commercials.

Here are a few warmup exercises that can be tailored to work as prompts for whichever emotion we're interested in.

Exercise: Full-Out 30 Seconds.

At a given signal, everyone in the room just lets rip and expresses the emotion as fully, physically and loudly as possible. After 30 seconds comes the signal (which probably needs to be visual) to stop. It's important to be clear that the actors shouldn't stick to the way they normally express an emotion in their own lives. If you happen to be a quiet-joy person, you need to find a way to holler.

It's easiest to do this one with joy. Most people are pretty comfortable with jumping up and down and hooting and high-fiving one another. Even if it's not their usual way of celebrating, they've seen enough of it to fake and enjoy it.

Anger is also pretty easy for most people, but some actors may have trouble. However, if one or two actors are quiet while a couple more tear around the room cussing a blue streak, it's usually enough to set the tone. If someone's really stuck, I might try giving her some paper to tear into shreds. Note: it's probably a good idea to specify that, even if your group is okay with a little light contact, no damage is to be done to people or furniture.

Sadness is harder. Some people get a lot out of sobbing and wailing while others either go quiet or can't help lapsing into "oh boo-hoo" parody. I find it helps to give people the option of expressing localized physical pain—and choosing an area of the body that seems most appropriate to their character in this particular scene. Is the pain in this scene more like a busted knee, a migraine or, say, a kick in the balls?

If you try this with fear, what you're looking for is pale-faced, trembling, shrieking terror. People will often say that that's not what they do when they get scared; again, remind them that their usual expressive pattern is beside the point. Most of us do everything we can to avoid fear. Becoming very still and quiet (freezing) is one such strategy, as are becoming angry (fighting) and withdrawing (fleeing). For the purposes of this exercise, you need to keep it big and loud, to express the fear rather than respond to it. If that expression results in some unavoidable secondary emotional response, such as anger or sadness, that's okay; but, if you can stand it, see if you can return to simple noisy horror.

Almost inevitably, trying the exercise with love leads to a lot of joking around. 30 seconds of full-out loooove. (Some touching okay, but no smooching or groping—also, this one doesn't have to be quite so loud.) Try it. Before starting, I like to suggest to the actors that, if they feel embarrassed, they try to embarrass **each other**. One way or another, the exercise will probably devolve pretty quickly into pure operatic silliness, but that's okay. What's really happening is that, in contemplating what it would be like to carry out the exercise sincerely, people see the opportunities to love one another, then, in terror, retreat into humor. Even completely failing at this exercise tends to have a positive effect on actors' ability to connect with each

other in a loving way on stage. It breaks the ice. After all, there's no
way the scene can be as embarrassing as the exercise.

———

Exercise: Inner Monologues.

Before the scene starts, each actor stands across from a partner and,
speaking in the character's voice, tells the story of the play up to this
point with a special emphasis on scanning for and enhancing a single
*emotion. Usually, it's best for the listener **not** to be another actor in the*
scene. Typically, I'll partner with one actor, ask the stage manager to pair
up with another, recruit an actor who is early for her scene as listener for
another, and so on. The exercise works best when you commit to full-out
*experience of the feelings (as in the **Full-Out 30-Second** exercises), but*
keep your voice down and mute your gestures as if you are talking in a
public place and don't want to make a scene. The listener's job is to look
the speaker in the eye, mimic his body language, and if necessary, give
the slightest prompt: "So, you're sad," or just "What else happened?"
There's a nice sense of conspiracy to this exercise, and people can get
quite worked up stealing sidelong glances over at the other actors as they
talk about their anger, sadness . . . or perhaps their secret love. . . .

Running the exercise in gibberish also works perfectly well, and
sometimes better.

In another variant, we run the exercise in gibberish and the
director acts as a kind of emotional conductor, indicating by gestures
whether the actors are to mostly contain, moderately contain, barely
contain or fail to contain the emotion.

———

EMOTION MEMORY: As discussed, as we try to uncover or amplify
emotion in the parts they are playing, I tend to steer actors more towards

using their imagination rather than their memory. Even if you are successful in recalling and re-experiencing the full strength of your sadness from when an old boyfriend broke up with you five years ago, how does that relate to the scene? In my experience, trying to hold on to the "boyfriend feelings" and somehow transfer them to the stage action is a non-starter.

However, I have had some luck with using emotion memory as a prompt, as a way for actors to simply remember what a particular emotion feels like. Then you go on stage, and rather than trying to carry the emotion with you, you scan for similar emotional responses as you play the scene in the moment. *This* moment, not five years ago.

Another tricky thing about the technique is that if it's not handled right, a session can become "therapy without a license." I'm not against people using theatre as therapy, but if a director or acting teacher asks an actor to reveal details of his personal life, that's over the line. It's not that a director should prohibit people from sharing their experiences, but it has to be clear that "opening up" is not compulsory. Not only that, if any actors do choose to share personal details, the director has to be sure not to over-praise their bravery or the ones who choose to keep to themselves may very well sit there feeling pressured and resentful.

So, if you're still interested after those cautions, here's how I've found it useful. In brief, the idea is to use your memory of the sensations that were part of a past event to evoke other details, including your emotional response to the event. Research suggests that in times of emotional excitement, the mind focuses intensely on the details pertinent to the event. In other words, our recall is likely to be extremely limited, but certain remembered details will be extremely vivid.

There's nothing extraordinary about the experience of using the senses to recall emotions—this isn't a past-life regression or anything. It's an everyday occurrence: you hear a song on the radio and the memory of a particularly happy summer day flashes to mind. For a moment, you re-experience a sense of well-being. Depending on your present circumstances, you may then continue to feel the slightest bit more joyful—or perhaps you feel a pang of nostalgia.

That's really all we're up to with this exercise:

Exercise: Emotion Memory.

After a brief relaxation meditation, you focus on an event from your past in which you felt one of the basic emotions very strongly. Sometimes everyone will work on the same emotion, sometimes different emotions. As best you can, you recall any sensations associated with the event: what you saw, heard, smelled, tasted, etc. If there was another person there, what did his face look like? What was the sound of his voice like? What were you wearing? What was the air like? The temperature? Can you recall anything about how you were sitting, standing, moving, etc.?

Now don't strain. You don't have to recreate the scene in its entirety or transport yourself through time so that you are "there." You're just looking for the details that produce the strongest emotional response in you. When you find one, don't hold onto it; just notice and let go.

Then everyone pairs up and chooses who will speak first and who will listen. Without actually telling the story of the past event, the speaker describes as many (or as few) of the emotionally evocative sensations as she cares to. You listen, mimic her body language, and pay attention to your own feelings—often, just attending to someone in this way is enough to trigger a response. When she's done, you switch.

❦

Note: With emotion memory, you have to be ready to take potluck. If you go after joy, half the time you'll end up with sadness. Recalling sadness can lead to anger at the way you were treated. Recalling fear can make you joyful. Pay attention to what's happening in the present: what you feel now is always more useful than what you felt five years (or five minutes) ago.

Other Variations

INCITING EMOTION: After you've done the emotion variations, as with the *Pick a Fight* variation below, try making the scene about the *other guy's* feelings. Instead of concentrating on what you are enjoying, try to show him a good time. Instead of focusing on your own pain, hurt him. Instead of amplifying your own fear, try to spook him. Instead of loving him, get him to love you.

EMOTIONS FROM YOUR CHARACTER'S PAST: You know in old movies when a character recalls a traumatic scene from her past and her voice immediately gets all quivery and shrill and. . . . You get the idea. This is a behavior, as far as I can tell, not found in nature but only on stage, screen and perhaps the odd mental ward.

When your character tells a story from her past, she may experience an echo of the feelings of yore. It's worth doing a variation in which, when your character recalls the experience, you scan for and enhance the emotions she probably felt at the time. But then bring the scene back to the present. Your character is telling the story for a reason in the here and now. It is almost always more realistic, and more effective, to have your character play down the emotional content of her reminiscences so that she can evoke the emotion in the *other* actor—and, not incidentally, in the audience.

PICK A FIGHT/BE POLITE: Conflict is exciting. A common mistake actors make is to dive into and play up the conflict instead of trying to avoid it. The truth is that most of us try to get along in our lives with a minimum of friction. See what happens if you magnify the conflict in the scene. Much as you did in the first *Anger* variation, use every excuse to pick a fight—the difference here is that you're trying to make the *other guy* mad. Then try the opposite: do your damnedest to get along (see the *Irony* variation below).

SELF-REGARD/SELF-CONTEMPT: I don't know about you, but I have days when I am just a terrific guy. And then I have days where I am lower (and less useful) than guano. Where in the scene does your character judge himself? Of course, any time you run the scene, you need to judge your progress, to pay attention to whether what you're doing is moving us towards realizing your objective. But it's also worth asking yourself how well the character happens to like himself at this moment. Characters self-evaluate.

Try a run of the scene in which you identify and amp up the character's self-contempt. Again, it's a bit like the anger variation except this time, every time you discover something wrong, all the blame comes back to you.

Then try another one in which you scan for and inflate the character's self-regard. This time the failures aren't as much of a big deal; the real you is in the successes.

IRONY: Does your character have a sense of humor about the situation—or at least a sense of irony? This time through, with every line you say, find at least one occasion to laugh. I'm not talking about yukking it up (as in the exercise below); the laugh has to be genuine for this to work. Usually, when you're on the right track, the laugh comes as just a slightest hint of a chuckle. This is a good one to run when the conflict in a scene is particularly vicious or the pain is especially grievous. You want to make sure that you have other options besides storm and stress. Don't lose the intensity; rather let the sense of humor/irony be the lid on the pressure cooker. Then maybe there's one line where you try to see the humor and *fail.* . . .

Exercise: Full-Out Laughter.

If you're having trouble doing the **Irony** *Variation, or you just need an energy boost, try laughing full-out for at least a minute. Yes, it's fake, but very often, as with yawning, if you fake it for a while the real thing takes over. Then, once the question changes from, "What are we laughing at?" to "What* **aren't** *we laughing at?" you're ready to do the* **Irony** *variation.*

TIME: What happens if you play the scene as if your character has to get what she wants within the next minute or it will be lost forever? Deadlines energize. It's also fun to have the other actor play the scene as if he's lining up a difficult putt on the final green in a crucial match: the stakes are high, but rushing is the last thing he wants to do.

CONDITIONS AND CONVENTIONS: Exaggerate, then minimize, the character's internal and external physical conditions. Go sloppy, falling-down drunk, for example—a 3% alcohol level—then try to play that level of intoxication but under control. Extend the stutter until the scene takes twice as long; then master it (almost) completely. Pain: upgrade the headache to a migraine, the toothache to a broken jaw, the scratch to a puncture wound; if the character has a death scene, put in every possible twinge, rattle and cough. Then keep that level of pain but try not to show it. The same goes for cold, heat, exhaustion.

You can play the same over/under game with stylistic conventions. If the language is full of imagery, for example, try physically enacting each picture; if you're doing Jaques' "seven ages of man" speech, for example, get up and *show* us the infant, the schoolboy, the lover, and so on. If, as in some Restoration comedies, the social customs are elaborately formal, make them absurdly so: bow twice as often and twice as low; where before you would strut, *prance*. If your character talks directly to the audience, each time you have an aside, go *sit* in an audience member's lap.

Then honor the convention by doing the opposite. Give us the seven ages without a single gesture, but still make us see the imagery. Play the social customs as lightly as you can, but don't dispense with them. Try to make the asides clear without breaking the scene at all.

OVERT/COVERT: A nice way to play around with opening the scene out: try the scene as if you are trying to broadcast your character's point of view to an unseen person eavesdropping (maybe even spying from) the next room—a room which happens to be beyond the fourth wall. Then try it as if you don't want the eavesdropper to hear (even though you're still loud enough to reach everyone in the rehearsal room).

CONNECTIONS: It's a good time to revisit the "listening" exercises from pages 52–53. *Interrupting* can shake up your pre-conceptions about cues, timing and delivery—in short, it can get you back in touch with the other actor if you're losing each other. Instead of *Back to Back*, try the scene with the usual blocking, but keep as much eye contact as possible; then try to keep the same connection (or make it even stronger) without looking at the other actor at all. Also, try *Echoes* again (where you find opportunities to mimic the other actor's body language), but this time, instead of focusing on your character's intention, orient towards figuring out what the *other guy* wants.

A couple of other ways to strengthen connection:

Exercise: Actors in Space.

Just for one run of the scene, throw out the blocking, forget the ground plan, and play the scene "in space." (I don't mean outer space—there's still gravity.) While there may be nothing wrong with the blocking or the set, sometimes if you can cut loose from them entirely—so that the only reality on stage is the other actor—you can make a more profound connection and perhaps even discover or re-discover what a scene is really about.

Exercise: Across the Gulf.

You and your partner stand on opposite sides of the room and stay there. Play the whole scene just trying to reach each other. Another version: he stands on the other side of the room with his back to you. Your objective is to get him to turn and face you.

Good. Do it again.

When I'm directing, I try to follow the physician's maxim, "First, do no harm." As I've said, I never try to run every variation for every scene we're working on; sticking to any system too long can gum up the works. Besides, once the scene has some serviceable blocking, actors will usually make plenty of discoveries just by running it over and over and over. Thus, my favorite direction for actors is, "Good. Do it again."

But my second favorite is, "Good. Try something else." If nothing else, I will usually run at least one variation that will tend to push the scene as far as it can go in the direction it is already headed, and one variation that will push the scene in a *contrasting direction*. Often, just playing two extremes is enough to bring out other contrasts. If it's a happy scene, try it sad. If it's a rip-roaring fight, try it as a love scene. You never know.

CHAPTER 5

Runthroughs: Hearts and Minds

I divided myself, as it were, into two personalities. One continued as an actor, the other was an observer. Strangely enough this duality not only did not impede, it actually promoted my creative work. It encouraged and lent impetus to it.

— Stanislavski, from *Building a Character*

THE PERFORMER'S DOUBLE CONSCIOUSNESS: Running longer sections of the play represents a new phase of the process and yet another radical shift in how we work. As you head towards performance, you're training yourself to adopt a split mind-set: you're going to need to play the character both from the inside and the outside simultaneously. For as long as actors have been writing about their stage experiences, they have described this peculiar state of mind (the phrase "double consciousness" is Henry Irving's). For example, as the veteran British actor, Sir Cedric Hardwicke, wrote:

On the stage [the actor] . . . becomes a dual personality. Outwardly he portrays the character he is supposed to represent. Inwardly the passions and emotions of his part occupy a kind of antechamber in his mind, while he remains in possession of the innermost room. . . . Great actors have raised this dualism to such heights of efficiency that, in the older days, they could count the house while playing the most taxing scene.

Writing in a similar vein, Joseph Chaikin calls the actor a "double agent." The heart is in the character, reacting to events spontaneously in real time, as if for the first time, but the head is strategizing about what comes next, making sure you don't peak too early, keeping variety in your tactics, monitoring your voice, etc. Or, as the nineteenth-century American actor, Joseph Jefferson, put it, "For myself, I know that I act best when the heart is warm and the head is cool."

STAND BACK: Since we began blocking, I've been playing fast and loose with the distinction between you and your character—and I hope you have too. Blurring the line between what is you and what is your character can be a useful strategy. You've been engaged in a process designed to help you get inside the character: to *identify* with her, to take her part. Right now, if everything has gone well, you're very close to the character. You see things from her point of view. You've got a good idea of how she thinks. Especially when you're playing variations on the emotional content of the role, it's handy to adopt the delusion that you *are* the character—or that the character actually exists within you.

But of course that's not literally true. She's fictional—not a person, but an illusion of a person. Now the task at hand has less to do with figuring out how your character sees the world than with how—in performance—the world is going to see her. Working with the director and the playwright, your job is to create an *effective* illusion. How will she *play*?

Actors often speak of their peak performing experiences as "getting lost in the part," but I think most people misunderstand what this actually means. The actor is never completely unaware of giving a performance before an audience. (You'd have to be psychotic to get *completely* lost in a role. I mean, come on, there are 300 people staring at you.) Though actors claim to be transported in this way, if you press them for details, some contradictions arise. For example, an actor might say he's forgotten the audience, but then talks about having the audience in the palm of his hand.

Anne Bancroft once said that the goal is not to be lost in a role, but to be *found*, to know exactly what you are doing at any moment: "It's a matter of thinking. Really, it's a matter of learning a thinking process. It's a matter of becoming aware of what it is you're doing, of what it is you're feeling, and then it's a matter of controlling it any way you want with your brain."

Right now, the best way to the core of the character is probably not to try to get closer but, ironically, to stand back. In all likelihood, some of your intuitions about how to play your part are right on, but others—even though they may feel right—aren't the best choices for the scene, the role or the play as a whole. Time to switch from feeling our way along to a more calculated approach, looking at the character from the outside. From now on, when I talk about "externals," I don't just mean the physical choices you make as part of performing the role; I mean anything you bring to the role from the outside, including your ideas about the role, your judgments, and your schemes about the most effective way to bring her story to the audience.

Moreover, there are some things about a character that you can't figure out from the inside. What the character wants or believes on the unconscious level is either so literally self-destructive, or so threatening to her conception of self, that if she were a real person, her mind would keep it hidden from her. If you were truly operating from inside the character, you would deny the existence of such intentions. When it comes to the unconscious, by definition, you can't get there from here.

By now, you probably have a pretty good idea of who your character thinks she is, but who do *you* think she is? What should the audience think and feel about her at the beginning of the show? What about at the end? Over the course of the performance, what do you want to *say* about her?

External Variations

When we were playing variations on individual scenes, you experimented with, among other things, expressing and containing emotion. In doing so, you were testing the limits of the part from the inside. Now that you're ready to start running longer sections of the play, and to focus more on fashioning an external characterization, let's continue the "variations" approach—in the first variation, trying new things and overplaying them, then underplaying them in the second—but on a larger scale.

When you're testing the limits on externals, it helps to experiment with an idea over multiple scenes, to get a feel for where it works, where it doesn't, where to pull out all the stops, where to tone it down, and how to fit it in with the progression and build of plot and character. That way, when you get into the final runthroughs before technical rehearsals, and the time comes to "set" the show—to put it in its final form—you'll be better prepared to create a dynamic, compelling, *complex* performance.

THE UNCONSCIOUS VARIATIONS: You know that moment, near the end of the horror movie, where the woman is alone in the house and she hears a noise in the basement? The creepy music starts. Everyone in the audience is thinking: "*No! Don't go down there! Go next door! Call 911!*" What does she do? Does she leave the house and go next door? Does she call 911? No, of course she doesn't. She goes down into the basement.

Why? Because she's curious? Maybe. But I don't think that's enough to explain it, do you? I wouldn't be *that* curious, would you? Because she's stupid? Well, again, maybe so, but how smart do you have to be to avoid that basement? Because the plot requires it? Also true (if a bit cynical), but that won't help you if you have to play the part.

I think she goes down to the basement because *that's what we all do*. At some point in our lives, no matter how smart we are, we go right into that basement.

When I was growing up, there was a girl who lived across the street who, one day, when she smelled gas, started to go looking for the leak with a box of matches. Fortunately, someone stopped her in time. What was she thinking? She wasn't a stupid person, nor was she suicidal exactly, but there were several similar incidents over the next couple of years. She was going through a rough patch at school—the usual teen angst—but I don't know that that quite explains it. Fortunately, she managed to survive and is no longer quite so accident-prone, but at the time, for whatever reason, she seemed to be in the grip of some unconscious urge towards self-destruction.

The most telling and disturbing—and sometimes the most moving—contradictions in your character may be between his conscious desires and those which remain unconscious. Where before you were working with his conscious intentions—which determine *how* he behaves—now is a good time to ask yourself *why* he behaves this way. Beneath his conscious desires, are there motives he would deny?

Look through the play and see if there are moments when you the actor can show us what you believe is going on at the deepest, least conscious level. To go back to an earlier example, if you've got an idea that one reason Iago destroys Othello is that he actually loves him (I'm not talking about repressed homosexuality here—though certainly some actors have interpreted the role that way), consider: are there places you can *show* us that tragic longing? If you did the "love variations," you may already have discovered some possibilities. On the other hand, if all you've felt towards him for the past few weeks is contempt, in the next runthrough keep an eye out for any opportunity to give us that contrasting side of the character. Perhaps at some point Iago unconsciously emulates—even imitates Othello's physical bearing. Perhaps it's just in the way he looks at Othello after his revenge is complete.

As a great "external" actor, Laurence Olivier frequently found ways to show his audience what was going on at level of the character's unconscious. His film portrayal of Hamlet is a good example. Shakespeare gives us a character who is at least concerned about, if not obsessed with, his mother's sexuality. Olivier pushes the Oedipal implications over the top; in his version, when Hamlet kisses his mother in her bedroom, that ain't no peck on the cheek. "Lead the audience by the nose to the thought," said Sir Laurence; when he had *ideas* about his character's unconscious, Olivier made darn sure we got them.

So plant some clues for the audience. As in the other variations, I think it's fun to start by taking the idea too far (plant a lot of big, obvious clues) so that you're really hitting people over the head. Then pull back: give us something more subtle. And when you set the show, make us think the stuff we're figuring out about your character is *our* idea.

VARIATIONS ON THEMES, SYMBOLS AND METAPHORS: Look back at the pre-rehearsal notes you took about the play. Think again about what's repeated, both within the scene you're working on, and throughout the play. What themes have emerged in the course of working on the show? Do you see any opportunities to add further repetitions? What symbols are important to the play and to this production? Can you find a way to emphasize or augment them? Is your character herself a metaphor? Does she (or do her actions) *stand for* something?

Example: In Moliere's *Tartuffe*, the father, Orgon, who is under the spell of a religious hypocrite, sincerely believes he is trying to bring his family to the path of salvation—by brute force if necessary. He preaches humility before God, but one could say that, unconsciously, he is actually putting himself in God's place. When I directed the show, there was a moment when Tartuffe had thrown himself on the floor and Orgon was helping him to stand up. The actors turned this mundane piece of stage business into a parody of the Creation of Adam from the Sistine Chapel—with Orgon in God's position.

Another Olivier film example: Shakespeare's *Richard III* makes repeated references to the title character as a monster; but Olivier's Richard is not just a figurative monster: check out that final scene, with Richard's body reflexively striking out with a sword five, six times *after* his death.

There's a glorious shamelessness to a death scene like that. Can you get away with something that big? What would it take to push the idea so far that the audience says, "Oh, come on now, *enough*"?

THE JUDGMENT (VILLAIN/HERO) VARIATIONS: Before rehearsals started, when you first read the play, you were able to look at the character from the outside and react, to pass judgment on the character—much as the audience will. Then you spent a whole lot of time trying not to judge, but rather to inhabit, his world. A few weeks ago, you may have been in better touch than you are now with what is astonishing or disturbing about him. You may have disliked him in some scenes, and with good cause. You may have found his manner absurd, his affectations ridiculous. Or perhaps you found him heroic in one scene and unbearable in another. Review your notes from before rehearsals started. And bring back the judgments— they'll serve you now.

Try a runthrough in which you bring out the very *worst* in your character. What does your character do that is petty, mean, stupid, or just against his own self-interest? What truth does he refuse to face? What flaw does he never admit to himself, or only admit to himself in retrospect after the climactic crisis of the play—perhaps once the harm he has caused is beyond remedy? Which of his tendencies tends to get him into trouble? Where does he get it *wrong*? Without losing the empathy you have gained for your character, play that *wrong* part up. If you can see that your character is blind to something, steer him right into the wall. If he loses friends and alienates people, make it worse.

Then, in another runthrough, bring out the very best in him. Where is he insightful, inspired, loving, self-aware? Where does he struggle with his difficulties? Where does he break through? Where does he get it right?

When you set the show, give us *both* people. Even if you end up playing 98% villain (or hero), give us that moment of contrast: that's where the character's humanity resides. And be mindful of how you want to seduce us (or alienate us) over time.

THE SIGNATURE VARIATIONS: Whether we admit it or not, most of us, attach a certain amount of importance to how we appear to others. We carry around ideas about which parts of our bodies—and which parts of our inner selves—are attractive or unattractive, and we try to accentuate the positive and eliminate the negative. Each day, we put on the costumes that we believe will most effectively support the story we want other people to tell about us: that we are efficient and professional, for example, or relaxed, or nonconformist, and so on. We adopt expressions, mannerisms, public personae. We choose the masks that we think best fit our "real" faces: not who we are, but who we *want* to be.

A mask is meant to be a device of concealment, not revelation: but often the masks we choose are the poorest kind of deception. Fearing detection, we choose the diametric opposite of the hidden face underneath and so give the game away to anyone with the slightest hint of imagination or taste for irony. The angel chooses a demon's face. The wolf becomes the lamb.

For all our efforts, in the end, our appearance is more a product of unconscious than conscious factors. First off, very few of us can completely and consistently project our chosen personae. Usually, little contradictions give us away: the nervous gesture, the sweat stain, the tension in the jaw— or perhaps the neatly pressed "casual" outfit. Moreover, the personae themselves are most often determined by factors and forces we are largely blind to: where we were born, how we were raised, forgotten childhood experiences, etc. In this sense, the personae *choose us.*

In seeking your character from the inside, you've undergone a process analogous to the conditioning each of us receives in the natural course of growing up and evolving a sense of self. With any luck, by now, you have some ideas about your character's physical way of being in the world, some of which may have originated in the "body shopping" exercises you did back when you started blocking. But some of your notions have probably arisen spontaneously, perhaps even unconsciously: the process of internalizing your character's circumstances, beliefs, desires and perceptions—not to mention speaking her words—has already led you to alter your physicality without realizing it. Perhaps, to your surprise, you find yourself speaking differently, holding your spine in a different position or using a "signature" gesture or vocal pattern quite different from your own. For example, if your character clearly has something to prove and is thus habitually emphatic, you may very well find yourself constantly jabbing a forefinger at your listener, as Stanislavski did when he played Ibsen's Doctor Stockman.

Creating the physical life of a role is one of the actor's juiciest opportunities to share a character's contradictions with the audience. You get to show us the discrepancy between the mask and the face, the persona and the person.

It would be nice if you could do one runthrough as the persona and another as the person, then sort out which one to play when, but things aren't that simple. You can't *just* play the person underneath, not if you're going to stick to the script: much of what she says and does is designed to mask that person. If she told the whole truth and nothing but, there would be no play. Similarly, trying to play the mask without the face beneath is also a nonstarter: the person is the whole reason for the mask.

So let's come at the problem from another angle. You've already had some practice exaggerating, then masking, your character's emotions. In so doing, you've likely already discovered that some of her emotions, though genuine, turn out to be masks for *other* emotions.

Now that you're ready to create a distinctive physical life for your character, choose a signature, a repeated gesture (or tic, or mannerism, posture, vocal pattern, rhythm, etc.) that you believe is characteristic of the person you are playing. Put aside for the moment the question of whether the gesture tends to reveal or conceal the truth about the character's inner life—we'll get to that later.

Do a runthrough in which you exaggerate the size and/or frequency of the signature. Go as far as you can without lapsing into self-parody. Then do another runthrough in which you suppress the signature—and, in a couple of key places, *fail to suppress it*. Take what is physically distinctive about the character and amp it up. Then, on the next round, try not to show it.

Some ideas:

- Take the image your character has learned to project and enlarge it. Then, keep the image in mind, but force yourself back closer to life-size.

- If you've got a strong image of your character as being like a particular animal, unleash it. Then rein it in.
- Pick a part of the body that you believe your character would tend to be proud of. Boldly feature that part at every opportunity. Then, while still flaunting it, try not to show that you're flaunting it—until that moment when you really *must* show everyone.
- Pick a part of the body that you believe your character would tend to be ashamed of. Do everything you can to cover it up or minimize it. In the first variation, don't be subtle: show us that you are hiding it. Then, next time, don't let on that you've got something to hide—until that moment when you're sure everyone is staring at you.
- If the character has learned a "correct" physical persona, make it hyper-correct. Then loosen up—except where you just can't help it. (Or tighten it up: some correct personae are elaborately casual.)
- Sometimes a character tries unsuccessfully to fit in with others who are of a different class, culture or group. On the first round, make shameless efforts and fail big. Next time, don't lose the desire to belong, but try not to get caught at it.
- If the character has a "tell" (any tic that reveals where she is vulnerable), repeat and magnify it until she gives away the game at every opportunity. Then make her a better poker player, but lose the crucial hand.

Mostly, people try to minimize their physical eccentricities. For example, when I make a conscious effort to adjust my posture, it is to *correct for*, not accentuate, my "natural" tendency to walk around with my head forward, my gut pulled in and my shoulders slightly hunched—like a human question mark.

And it's not just bad habits we try to suppress: we unconsciously play down *anything* that would distinguish us from the people around us. When I'm in a room full of people who speak in a particular accent or a rhythm different from my own, I'll often notice myself starting to echo their vocal patterns. Around macho guys, I swagger a little. I don't *decide* to do this exactly; it happens before I know it. This is one reason why when you choose a trait, you should consider showing its opposite. Otherwise you're just cartooning. Ultimately, you're looking to calibrate your character's physical eccentricities to each situation and relationship she encounters. We aren't one thing all the time; put us in a different crowd, and we change.

Yes, we are all yearning to be recognized as individuals, and so we do things to make ourselves distinctive. But in moments of crisis, given the choice between standing alone at the heroic frontier and attaining full membership in the tribe, most of us opt simply to belong. Rather than expressing our individuality by building our own cabin in the wilderness, we'll settle for personalizing our cubicle, thank you.

Even when people are trying to stand out, they usually don't want to be *caught* at it. Shaw's Joan of Arc may know at some level that she aspires to greatness, martyrdom, even sainthood, but she still maintains the fiction that she is only a simple country girl doing what she is told.

Ironically, at least in the world of the stage, if a character is consciously trying to fade into the woodwork, that's when she'll most likely manifest her individuality. Even a person who has been trained, or has trained herself, to speak and move according to a group's particular set of rules—to comport herself with military bearing or charm school correctness, for example—will behave idiosyncratically under the stress of the *plot.*

PLAY IT STRAIGHT: Having explored the limits of both the character's masks and his "tells"—and the ways in which he tries to stand out or to blend in—when it comes to setting the show, you and the director are going to have to decide what balance to strike. Usually, as with emotion, something close to the "suppressed" physical variation will serve you best—because the very act of suppressing *anything* suggests both the mask and the face, both persona and person. Most characters are undercover agents; the person you are playing is himself playing a role. Like a spy in enemy territory, the last thing he wants is to be discovered. As a rule, make your character a good liar, perhaps even good enough to fool himself, but not quite good enough to fool the audience—not *all* the time, anyway. It almost never hurts to underplay something—as long as you *have* something to underplay—then find the best place to blow your cover.

OR NOT. If you're doing flat-out parody or Monty Python-type sketch comedy, to hell with subtlety. Some roles (usually they are small "character" parts) *demand* unconstrained weirdness. Your character may be physically outrageous, off-the-charts eccentric, completely over the top. Enjoy your time in outer space.

Set and Simplify

As we come to the final runthroughs before tech, it's time to put our house in order before we invite the audience in. Some directors call this *setting* the show. It's a useful way to start thinking about the work: not that we're going to set it in concrete, but that the choices we're making from here on out will determine more or less what the audience sees. Even though, with any luck, the cast will never stop making new discoveries and subtle shifts—rediscovering the show—the object now is to create something stable, rooted, cohesive.

So how, out of all the possibilities we've generated in rehearsal, are you supposed to make the right choices? How do you know what to keep and what to toss? How do you know which word to stress? Where should you tread lightly? Where should you come on full force? Is your physical characterization enough, too much or just right?

It's as if you've created a huge audio mixing board with all kinds of levers and switches. Now, before the concert, it's time to actually set some levels.

If I were to continue the analogy, of course, the director would be the sound man working the levers and you'd be the musician up on stage, but it doesn't quite work that way. Of course, the director will help you. But directing you in the part is not the same as playing the part. She'll give you notes about where you need to crank it up and where you need to ease off.

If you forget things, she'll remind you. She can tell you the effect she wants. She can tell you when you're getting closer and further away. If there's something out of tune, she may even be able to diagnose what it is. But she can't fix it for you. In the end you have to set your own levels. How are you supposed to do that and play the music at the same time?

To my mind, the best way to collaborate with your director at this moment is to keep your focus on two of the most basic elements of the play. Keep your mind on showing us what happens, and put your heart into living your character's wants. Do that, and much of the rest will sort itself out.

TELL YOUR CHARACTER'S STORY. There are all kinds of dynamics, tricks, and techniques involved: effective storytelling means watching the build, creating suspense, keeping our attention, dropping clues, keeping things lively, varying tactics, making promises, and ultimately delivering the goods. But if you try to keep all of those things in mind, it's going to be hard to do *any* of them.

So relax. Just show us what your character does and what happens to him. You know how. You've seen and heard so much story-telling; it's practically a part of your genetic code. You know those people who just seem to have a talent for telling stories? So do you. If you've ever made someone laugh by telling her what happened to you, you've got a feel for it. You find yourself exaggerating some details and leaving others out. You create a semi-factual narrative of what was going on in your mind. You play with people's status, and with your own. And, if you're at ease with your listener, you do all these things quite unconsciously.

What will make you an effective performer in this role now is no longer a question of technique. Nor is it about making the "right" choice at the right time. Forget the details. You're seeking a state of mind now. Keep cool.

While the storyteller keeps cool, the character is on fire—from the very first to the last moment of the play, she is driven by a single burning desire.

By now you know all kinds of things about your character's world, her language, her relationships, her thoughts, her intentions, her emotional life, her motivations. You've explored the dynamics of the part—how far you can crank it up, and how far you can turn it down. You've got some idea of the structure of the role, how you want the audience to feel, what you want to reveal and what you want to suppress. Et cetera, et cetera.

In short, you know too much. Simplify.

As you prepare to perform the show, you need to let go of all the work you have done in rehearsal and trust that you will remember what you need to when the time comes. Like playing music, or hitting a golf ball, acting requires a series of lightning fast choices and adjustments so fine that the conscious mind cannot reliably execute them. After sinking a perfect putt or hitting a perfect drive, champion golfers, asked to recall what they were thinking at the time, universally respond: "Nothing." Amateurs, by contrast, are thinking about the mechanics of their performance. It's not that the mind is never engaged: before the swing, the professional golfer surveys the lay of the land, chooses the appropriate club, etc. But he is very clear about his point of attention: between the shots, he sets the goal; during the shots, he relies on what he has practiced.

THE SPINE: To navigate your way through the play, you need a clearly-stated, simple goal, a point of orientation like the golfer's flag on the green, or the mariner's North Star. What is your character seeking from the very first moment of the play until the very last? Sometimes called the super-objective or through action, the *spine* is the sum of all her actions, desires, efforts, intentions, objectives. For the duration of the play, it is her reason for being.

Go for the most obvious answer. Sometimes, the spine is quite literal. If you are trying to save the farm throughout the whole play, that's great. That's probably all you need to remind yourself of right now.

Just as often, however, the character's attention will shift from one physical objective to another—or from an objective that's easy to articulate in literal, physical terms to one that is more abstract or internal. If you were trying to save the farm in Act I, but now, in the second act, the farm's gone, what the heck are you doing on stage?

Let's say you're playing Dorothy in *The Wizard of Oz* (I know, it's not Madame Ranevskaya, but bear with me). How do you reconcile her desire to run away from home with her desire to return? Okay, Oz isn't her kind of place, and she misses her family. But what is it that makes the departing Dorothy the same person as the returning? The way you answer that question will not only help you keep your bearings when the monkeys are on the wing, it will also sum up and solidify your *interpretation* of the character. If, for example, you emphasize that what starts the play is Dorothy's displacement from the safe haven of childhood, if Dorothy experiences the testiness of the adults around her as an *expulsion* from the home she loves, then maybe the whole show is about looking to regain a sense of home. As a child, she runs away to find a home; as an adult (having killed the witch) she comes back to claim a new place in her old home. So you focus on: *home.* And it helps you sing "Somewhere Over the Rainbow," figure out what's up with the munchkins, liquidate the witch *and* play that sappy ending with genuine feeling.

You need a simple idea that links all that complex stuff together. You'll know when you've got a winner: a good answer will feel solid, right, reassuring when you get hold of it: "*Oh, is that all I have to do? Okay, I can do* ***that***." You can use it as a mnemonic, a mantra, a reminder to keep your eyes on the (character's) prize. More importantly, a good answer will *stir* you; it will call you to action.

Repeat it to yourself before your next runthrough. In terms of playing your character, it's all you need to carry with you on stage. So check your fly, remind yourself of your first line, then go play.

"Bigger, Louder, Faster, Funnier"

I remember when I first heard a director give this piece of "standard" end-of-the-rehearsal-period direction. It must be pretty old, because the way he spoke it, it was clear that the phrase not only had quotation marks around it but was in an antique font.

Nonetheless, it's sound advice for the short, giddy phase right before tech. I'm not sure how to describe this period exactly, except as a kind of pumping up. The adrenaline is really starting to flow, and we have to find a way to channel it productively. It's also our last chance to make sure that we know what we're doing and that the show will actually reach the audience.

First priority is to double-check that everything can be seen, heard and understood (the bigger/louder part). Then there's the matter of picking up cues. You don't want to move or speak faster, per se—indeed, sometimes the way to catch an audience's attention is to *slow* your speech—but you do want to make sure that the beginning of your line comes before the sound of the other guy's last word has died away. This is one of the ways that stage dialogue differs from ordinary speech. Unless there is a deliberate pause, the rule is: no dead air. And don't pause in anticipation of laughs; no one knows where an audience is going to laugh. If a director tells you different, honor the direction for now, but be ready to toss it at a millisecond's notice in performance.

As for the "funnier" part, my sense of what that means is, paradoxically, that you have to find ways to take a comic role even *more seriously*. As Jack Sydow, my mentor in grad school, used to intone: comedy is serious business. The straighter you play it, even as the show gets more and more outrageous, the funnier it will be.

But there's another aspect to "funnier," and it has something to do with having some fun with the show and with each other. In the best pre-tech rehearsals, people tend to share a joyful determination to drill anything that needs drilling within an inch of its life. At the same time, we need to let off steam. A certain amount of self-parody can actually serve both purposes.

Exercise: Speedthrough (Runthrough al Italiano).

You're going to run the show as loud and as big and as fast as you possibly can. The stage manager readies his stop watch, and the director yells: "Ready, set, GO!" You talk like a 33 1/3 RPM record (remember those?) turned up full blast and set on 45 RPMs—78 RPMs if you can manage it and still articulate your words. Where you made a little, subtle gesture before, now it's HUGE. Where before you wept quietly, you break into great loud snorty sobs. Where before you walked, now you DASH around the stage. Where before you just sat on the sofa, now you make a dive for it.

The best time to do this exercise is at one of the very last rehearsals just before tech—not the last one (you want a good, serious run in that one), but the second to last. It's amazing how much a show can gain from this exercise, and I've never seen a cast lose anything by doing it. It's a great deal of fun, and it helps everyone to realize just how much they actually can pick up their cues if they've a mind to. But most importantly, if there's something about the show that's become overly tight or *precious*, a speedthrough can help everyone loosen it up a bit.

When the speedthrough is done and everyone's lying gasping on the floor, I usually recommend this:

Exercise: Blank Slate.

On the morning before your last runthrough before tech, as soon as you wake up, read the play. Pretend you've never read it before. Pretend you're sitting in the audience hearing the lines for the first time.

Do this again on the day before the show opens.

CHAPTER 6

Tech: It's Not About You

Here's a typical tech rehearsal routine:

- **Dry Tech:** The designers, crew, and director get the cues ready without the actors.
- **Wet Tech (Cue to cue):** As in dry tech, we do the lighting and sound cues, but this time, we add the actors. Where there's a cue, we run the lines and blocking around it over and over until the timing is reasonably accurate. We run as little of the show as possible.
- **Stop and Go:** It's more or less a runthrough, but again, the emphasis is on getting the cues right. We might skip some parts and run other parts *ad nauseam*.
- **First Dress Rehearsal:** Some acting might happen, but it's mostly about putting on the clothes, looking at them under the lights, and figuring out any quick changes. Usually, we stop only if something is so screwed up that it doesn't make sense to continue.
- **Second Dress:** As close as possible to performance conditions minus the audience. Generally, unless the show is particularly simple from a technical standpoint, the actors are still getting used to all the new elements, and the tech crew is still refining their timing.

- **Preview**: We add the last element: an audience. Technically, it's supposed to be a rehearsal, but everybody knows it's really a performance.

For actors, tech, especially the early parts, can be an enervating, crashing bore. Expect not only that there may be long periods in which you will have to just stand and wait (sometimes for no reason that you can discern), but that throughout these times you will be required to stay on your toes and respond *immediately* to the stage manager's instructions. What's more, under pressure of time, all those people (the director, designers, et al) who were so nice to you previously may now seem a little bit *testy*, okay?

When I'm acting, I find it's helpful to notice how little of tech is about me. It also helps to remember how much everyone else has invested in the show, and how frightening it is for everyone that their work is about to go in front of an audience. Having acted for most of my life, I know that all the actors' performances will go flat as soon as we hit the theatre. Nothing to be done. It happens every time. Also, bear in mind that no matter how efficient the tech process actually is, it always *seems* inefficient to actors. My tech mantra, which I mutter under my breath all through these final rehearsals is: "Nothing is broken."

Trust the techies. They're working as fast as they can. Trust the director; she can see things you can't. Trust the designers—especially the costume designer—they're doing everything they can to make you look good (or, if not good, *right*). Report problems (especially safety problems), but try not to get shrill.

Be nice to everyone, especially your stage manager; at this moment, she may be under more pressure than anyone. Set your sights on being generous: with your time, with your attention, with your praise, with your compassion. Bring food to share (but don't eat in costume). And if the tension and boredom really start to get to you, try this: see who else in the room seems rattled or out of sorts. Take extra care to be kind to that person. Especially if he doesn't deserve it.

Keep your wits about you. Stay loose. Meditate. Drill your lines. Breathe. It will get better.

CHAPTER 7

Performance: Honorable Intentions

HERE'S WHAT USUALLY HAPPENS. The first time the show goes in front of people, almost everything gets better. There may be a few cues out of place, a dropped line or two. Maybe the show is a little raw, but if so, the audience seems to be eating it up without noticing. Scenes that never really quite worked before now blossom into life. Moments that were always a little bogus are suddenly filled with real feeling and depth. The most marginal singer in the chorus is, halleluiah, *on pitch*!

Performers refer to this minor miracle as being "*on.*" To be *on* is to be completely absorbed in the task at hand, to feel the part deeply, to enjoy it profoundly, to know, just know that the audience is right there with you. When you are on, performing is easy, a pure pleasure, a holy thing. Every choice seems new and fresh, every moment is a discovery. You feel as though you never understood the part until now, not really. After the curtain call, everyone goes home exhilarated and relieved.

The next night, the show tanks. Let's talk about why.

One reason opening night (or preview) tends to go so well is related to the phenomenon we've all heard about in which, in order to free her child, a 120-pound mother lifts a 4,000-pound car off the ground. Once the kid is safe, she faints. Adding an audience stimulates the release of some major chemicals. When that cocktail hits the bloodstream, actors are suddenly able to play their roles with astonishing energy and insight.

Adrenaline allows us to do some amazing things, but the state we can achieve under its influence is, unfortunately, not permanent (otherwise post-trauma, any time she had a flat tire, mom would be able to just hoist up the car and fix it without using a jack). But their freakishness and transience don't make "adrenaline strength" or adrenaline consciousness any less real. We all have super powers. Unless you believe that every time they do their job well actors are assisted or possessed by supernatural forces, there's no other explanation. We have outlandish capabilities; we just don't always know how to tap into them.

Nonetheless, after the rush of the first night, actors tend to expect that they'll be able to go right out and do the same thing again. Mistake. Like Wile E. Coyote looking down and discovering there's no longer ground under his feet, the actor realizes the energy isn't there. The chemical boost is gone. And while the audience may be just as responsive (at least at first) as the previous night's, they aren't responding to the same things in the same way. The actor tries to re-capture the feeling of last night, and to play up the parts that worked so brilliantly. Bigger mistake.

And then, things start to really go wrong. And not just with a single actor; it seems as if a plague has infected the cast and crew. Some may be sicker than others, but everyone feels it and everyone suffers. Whole passages get dropped, entrances and cues missed; people may even be injured.

As a director, on the day after the first good performance, I used to come to the theatre in foul mood. Partly, this was born of despairing that the show that night would be any good. Partly, I was conscious of wanting to use my grim reaper imitation to scare the cast back into an adrenalized state. Sometimes the strategy worked—at least for that night—but I knew that I was just putting off the inevitable. Without a reliable *replacement* for adrenaline, without an alternative energy source, the show is bound to crash before it stabilizes—and then to have occasional relapses all the way through the run.

THE ON/OFF SWITCH: If there were one (and if we could reach it), we'd probably have to keep flipping it back on like an overloaded circuit breaker. When actors talk about individual performances in retrospect, they say things like, "I was *on* tonight, but I was more *on* last night, don't you think?" Or, "I think I was somewhat *off* tonight in the second act, but more *on* than the matinee—anything would be more *on* than that, right?" Even the best performances are off some of the time. The actor gets distracted, wanders, and brings himself back. The nights when he's *on*, he's just managed to keep the juice flowing more consistently. The night's when he's *off*, he's standing there in the basement whacking at the fuse box with a sputtering flashlight.

Actors live under the perpetual threat of banishment to this basement. We know it will happen, but we don't know when, and we don't know how long we'll be down there. Thus, we are a superstitious people. Many of us carry lucky charms. Instead of wishing each other good luck, we say, "break a leg"—a kind of reverse psychology in use against malicious sprites since medieval times. Because *Macbeth* has acquired the reputation of carrying with it an unusually high incidence of theatrical disasters, the very mention of "the Scottish play" in a theatre is taboo.

We are in danger. We see the tremendous risk, the hubris of our profession; we know how voracious our own ego is. And, especially after a good ego-feeding performance, the jitters start: we know we will be punished. Whatever its true origin, I like to think of the expression, "break a leg" in light of the myth of Icarus. If we think of actors as our astronauts, sailing ever higher each performance, courting the gods' punishment by soaring into the light—then perhaps wishing them a broken leg is a way of saying, "when you fall, I hope that at least it's not fatal."

ORIENTING TO THE AUDIENCE: Sometimes it seems to a cast that an off night originates not with the cast itself, nor with hostile gods or sprites, but with the audience. This is particularly the case in comedy. When the audience is silent, the fun goes out of playing the show. In fact, the audience may be sitting there on the other side of the lights smiling their heads off, enjoying every moment of the show, but the actors don't know this. So in their disappointment and anger, the actors imagine a sea of hostile faces staring up at them or worse, *not* staring at them but nodding off instead. They imagine that tonight, by some mathematical fluke, the average IQ of the audience has plummeted, or that everyone is too stuck up or drunk to laugh, or that the theatre management has secretly arranged a Wednesday-night discount for the humor-impaired.

But even if any or all of these things were somehow to come true, the fact is that, for the most part, we as actors *create* our audience. If we are hostile, the audience becomes hostile. If we are joyous, our joy is infectious. If we have lost our sense of humor, the audience isn't going to be able to locate it. If we are reverent, the auditorium will become a sacred space.

Indeed, the other reason why an actor improves when you put him in front of an audience is that doing so tends to yank him out of his single-minded concentration on playing the character and to pitch him headlong into the state of dual consciousness. While his heart remains (at least somewhat we hope) in character, his mind is shouting, "Oh my God, people are looking!" In short, once you shove him out on stage, he remembers why he is there.

And, like a man who has at last managed to ask an intimidatingly beautiful woman out to dinner, he is on his best behavior. He woos the audience. As an actor, he gives them, not a false self, but his best self— *sharing* his performance *with* the audience rather than keeping it to himself or hitting them over the head with it. He doesn't let his trivial worries and aches interfere with his desire both to shine and to please. He watches himself. And, at the same time, he *listens* to the audience and responds intuitively to their moods, their needs, their hungers.

When the actor's performance tanks on the second night, it is as if, on a subsequent date with the same woman, she no longer laughs at all his jokes, so he either becomes *so* desperate to please that she can't help but start questioning her judgment in going out with him in the first place, or he says the hell with her and mumbles and grunts his way through the rest of the evening until he can go home and have a stiff drink.

"Consciousness," according to the neuroscientist, Antonio Damasio, "allows the player to discover if the strategy is correct, and in case it isn't, to correct the strategy." In their disappointment, the "off night" actor, and our easily-wounded Romeo have in common an inability to self-evaluate and self-correct. This isn't just a loss of confidence; it's an impairment of *consciousness*: namely, the state of dual consciousness (the ability to be both in the moment and above the moment) that is essential to the performer.

By contrast, the conscious man, out on the same date, even if he isn't having as good a time as the night before, will respond to the woman he's with and stay in relationship. Indeed, if makes a commitment to be with her long term, when she is in an ugly mood, he may even learn—without compromising himself—to respond to her lovingly *because he has created an intentional relationship with her*. It's not the high of a first date, but it can be deeper and more satisfying. And it's certainly a heck of a lot more dependable.

On an *off* night, the actor has, in effect, lost track of his intended relationship with the audience. Indeed he may have unintentionally created a *hostile* relationship: to the actor, the audience has become a pack of philistines incapable of appreciating him; or perhaps he is playing to an infestation of garden slugs. Or perhaps he has committed himself (and us) one of the many lose-lose games people play to punish one another: he is starving and we won't give him a crumb. . . .

When you are preparing to perform for an audience, in order to get into the proper state of concentrated attention, neither lost in the role nor distracted from it, you need to orient yourself both to the task at hand and to the audience. You've already learned to sum up the task at hand in terms of the character's spine. But how can you sum up your intended relationship with the audience? As with any relationship, you can't dictate what the other person is going to do, but you can get straight how you want to regard them, what you want from them, and what you want for them.

You cannot wait for the first laugh to get you going. You cannot depend on adrenaline to carry you along. When an actor learns how to reliably and consistently create (and re-create and re-invent) an intentional, positive relationship with the audience *before he even sets foot on stage*, the result is that he is almost always *on*. And, in any given moment of performance, when he finds that he is *off*, he has the ability to calmly correct his course, shift his relationship with the audience back to firmer ground, and carry on with renewed poise and energy.

So, okay, maybe some members of this Sunday matinee audience *aren't* the brightest crayons in the box. But, today, they're *your audience*. As the man says, the fault is not in our stars, but in our selves. So let's get to work.

What Are You Doing on Stage?

AN INTENTIONAL RELATIONSHIP: Back when you were still adjusting to the blocking, any time you were struggling with a scene, you tried to articulate your character's intention towards the other character in the scene. Who is he to you, and what do you want from him? Formulating an intention is probably the most universally applicable and effective practice that actors have come up with in the last century. You've used it to clarify and intensify your interaction with the other actors.

Then, when you wanted to further strengthen your intention towards the other actor, you added imaginary or analogous circumstances to the scene; you played the scene *as if* those circumstances were true. In doing so, your playing gained momentum and emotional intensity because, having prepared yourself in this way, you endowed both the other person and the circumstances with a significance that was of your own making. You made the scene mean something to you.

Why shouldn't you do the same with respect to your audience? Who are they to you, and what do you want from them? And what does performing this role for this audience *mean* to you?

When you set an intention for yourself as the character, it wasn't just a random choice; you were guided by the given circumstances. Likewise, in choosing an intention for yourself as a *performer*, you have circumstances to draw on, in this case, the givens of your own life and personality. If this sounds daunting, it needn't be. After all, you've had a lot of experience with yourself, and probably some exposure to how you behave in high-pressure situations such as performing for an audience.

It doesn't take a lot of navel gazing to figure out, given your life history, what your tendencies are. You probably have some idea of what you, at your best, are capable of and what you aspire to. Likewise, you've got a sense of how low, at your worst, you have actually sunk—and, if you're like me, you've got a reasonably vivid picture of how low you might go if your descent remains unchecked. In short, you are capable of being your own hero or your own villain. You've got a higher self and a lower. Let's start by formulating an intention that will summon that higher self to action.

To review, the components of an intention:

- A desire: *What do I want for this audience?*
- A relationship: *Who are they to me?*
- An objective: *How will I know when I'm reaching them?*
- An obstacle: *What's in my way?*

DESIRE: There's a moment in the movie *Superman* where Lois Lane asks Superman why he's here, and he earnestly replies, "I'm here to fight for truth, justice, and the American way." The way Christopher Reeve deadpaned the old comic book line, the implication is, "Isn't *everybody?*" He's right: having a higher calling may be what exalts us and compels us nobly to strive for the greater good, but it's also no big deal. Everybody's got one.

Whether or not you've ever articulated it to yourself, you already have a *credo*, a sense of the higher purpose of your acting, a reason you *believe in* what you are doing. Stella Adler said that part of actor's job is to "recognize that life is important, not casual." When you stand in front of that audience, what do you stand for?

Look back at the notes you took on first encountering the play. It may be that reminding yourself of what the play is about will be enough to clarify your purpose with respect to the people who are going to come see it. What does this play say that people need to hear? What part do you have to play in bringing this news, this message? What does to play show us? Or maybe it doesn't have anything in particular to say, but then what is it supposed to do for us? Will it disturb us? Reassure us? Divert us? As William Ball says, choose a good "actable" verb, something you can put your shoulder behind.

Whether or not the play itself gives you a sufficient reason for being on stage, it's worth taking a look at what you, as an actor stand for *in general.*

I know it sounds both corny and snobby, but if it works for you to be the bearer of *Art* to the culturally impoverished masses, do that. Or maybe your role is to bear witness, to show us who we are, or who we might be. Or do you love theatre because you believe that when we gather in a room to share in the experience, we are better for it? Or are you providing people with escape? Or are we all asleep, and it's your job to wake us up—perhaps gently, but with cold water if necessary? Are you making everyone's life more colorful? To what or to whom are you dedicating yourself, your life, your performance?

Hunt around a bit. You'll know when you've got the right idea. As you did when you first explored your role, you may want to pay particular attention to what about acting in general—or about acting this role— moves you towards tears or outrage. If you can get past the embarrassment of being an enthusiast (you know: the inner voice that says sarcastically, "Oh, listen to *him*, will you?"), you may find a hidden strength of purpose in those emotions.

Maybe you're not sure why you're here, but there's no reason to let that stand in your way. You don't need absolute certainty to take on a sense of purpose. You're an *actor.* You can try things on and see what fits you best. And you don't need to lose your sense of humor about it either. We're talking about a reason to get up in the morning (or, for you night owls, the afternoon), a joyful thing. Determination does not have to be grim. And there are few things worse than going to a performance where the prevailing ethic seems to be: "We've suffered for our art; now it's your turn."

Nor do you have to be selfless: so, okay, you love the attention, but maybe that means that what you have to give us involves shining brightly as an example—so that others can feel freer to do the same. Okay, so you're doing this show because it's the one that will pay the bills (and bully for you if you've found such a job), but why else *might* you do it? However selfish your motives on one level, if you can incorporate some aspect of service to others into your work, it will tend to counteract whatever tendencies towards self-absorption you may possess. Yes, you're up there for you, but you're also up there *for them.* And if you can find a way to come from a place where you don't just want something *from* your audience, you genuinely want something *for* them, you will arrive in that realm of dual consciousness actors call being *on.*

RELATIONSHIP: Let's assume that—even if they don't yet know it—the audience *needs you.* Here's the beauty part: most of the time, you don't know a lot of particulars about the people watching you. Since they could be *anybody*, you're free to invent an identity for them. This doesn't mean that formulating a relationship with your audience is an arbitrary or uninformed process. Again, you do have a notion of what you and your play have to offer.

What's your angle? What does your audience need from you? Have we come to see you because we take ourselves too seriously, so we need a good Malvolio to make fun of (then feel sorry because we treated him so badly)? Are too quick to dismiss the still small voice within, so we need a Saint Joan to show us what it would take to follow it? When you do Richard III, can you get us to admit that, even though we pretend to be "nice," we're getting off on how bad you are?

James Nicola calls the practice, "casting your audience." Who are we to you? To my mind, the most effective intentional relationships have a status differential built in. Usually it's only a slight difference. Say, for example, you're trying to loosen them up. Better to think of them as a bit shy (but secretly on the wild side) rather than treating them as Easter Island statuary. Another example: say the play you're doing has a political slant. If your first impulse is to go out there and slap some sense into these idiots, you might want to pause and consider formulating another approach. What if you assume the audience is bright, interested and even informed—but they may not have considered *this* angle on the issue? You may be planning to shock them a bit, but consider seducing them first. You'll have a better time, and so will they.

Some plays seem at first glance to demand a maximum status gap between actor and audience. For example, on the surface, the fun of (the whole point of) playing the title role in Durang's *Sister Mary Ignatius Explains It All for You* is that you cast the audience as school children, then go out there and terrorize us. But in such cases, there is almost always an implicit relationship between actor and audience that undercuts the literal relationship between the character and the audience. Rather than actually holding the audience in contempt, the actor playing Sister Mary conspires with us to hold *Sister Mary* in contempt.

As Nicola points out, any time you step on stage, you are asking your audience to be co-conspirators with you in the creation of a fictional world. The fact that you know at least a little more about this world than we do makes you not just our host but our guide. However you choose to think of us in the audience—as frightened children, as soldiers in the battle, as fellow travelers—find a way to welcome and enjoy us. Reveal your world a glimpse at a time ("Did you see *that*? Well, what about . . .wait for it, wait for it . . . what about *this*?). The experience you are having is extra-ordinary; it is not life as usual. Create a relationship with the audience in such way that we cannot help but *join you.*

OBJECTIVE: As when you were formulating your character's intention for a scene, it can help you strengthen your intention towards the audience if you give yourself a goal, a concrete payoff, an objective—some picture you can hold in your mind of what success would look like. However, while your character's objectives are generally short term, your credo as an actor should have a longer reach. Of course, at any given moment during the show, you want to make 'em laugh, make 'em cry, make 'em think, etc.—and then you want a standing ovation. But you've set yourself a higher goal, one that extends beyond the curtain call.

So here's the question to answer: When your audience leaves the theatre after the show, how will you have made a difference in their lives (or maybe just their evening)? If you were somehow able to accompany someone from your audience home after the show, how would it be clear to you that the experience had really gotten under his skin? How do you know when you've won? Can you see it in your mind's eye? Maybe you want people to go home arguing about the politics of the play—or maybe you want them to march out of the building, take to the streets and start the revolution (look, it's a *fantasy*; why not?). Or maybe your wish is for all the couples in the theatre, especially those who have been taking each other for granted, to be filled with sudden tenderness and say sloppy sentimental things to one another. Maybe you want the quiet women to speak up. Maybe you want the people who secretly fantasize about being pop stars to hit the karaoke bars.

OBSTACLE: In general, actors don't choose to have tough audiences. When you were formulating obstacles for your character, you wanted maximum resistance. The more your character has to push against, the higher the stakes, and the more energy in the scene. By contrast, as an actor trying to reach your audience, you're looking to recognize, then *minimize* their obstacles. (We'll talk more about *your* obstacles in a minute.)

Accordingly, there is a special psyching-up an actor needs to do in advance of playing for what promises to be a tricky audience. Remember first of all, there's great strength to be found in welcoming a challenge. While it's a treat to perform for a full house of your loyal, literate Saturday night subscribers, there can be a special pleasure in taking on the Sunday pay-what-you-will matinee.

When you know the show is a hard sell, rather than just playing your usual game harder, you need to be willing to shift your tactics a bit. Rather than blaming your Sunday matinee audience for not being your Saturday night audience, see if you can find out some particulars about who exactly they are, and use the knowledge to advantage: find a way to *love* that they've come to see you. If you are genuinely enthused about who they are, you'll find ways to reach them.

If you know the blue-haired ladies come Sunday afternoons, remember that not only are they a little deaf, they're also whip-smart. Let your playing be loud and lean: cut to the chase—they'll probably understand more about the play than you do. If you doing a special performance of *Hamlet* for incarcerated felons, don't pretend this show is business as usual. When you talk about Elsinore as a prison, don't betray the people watching you by denying where you *are*. If you know that today's audience for *Angels in America* will be full of (quite possibly homophobic) teenagers on a school trip, remember what it is like to be that age: uncertain who you are, vulnerable, bluffing your way through. What do you and your play have to offer *them*?

When your audience is unexpectedly taciturn (or inappropriately exuberant), it helps to have a few positive explanations up your sleeve. So they're quiet? Ah, they're *listening*! So they're rude? Ah, someone to *spar with*! The play must be *provoking them*! So there's not many of them? Ah, *intimacy*! (You need to give them something to tell their friends, don't you?) I know such relentless optimism sounds a bit silly, but really what other choice do you have? Sulking won't help anybody.

There are some plays that would be tough for any audience. Back when you were cast, you probably already had some notion of whether your audience would buy what you have to sell right away (you're doing yet another revival of the theatre's hit production of *A Christmas Carol*), or whether they would need some convincing (you're doing, say, some really wiggy Strindberg-type thing).

If you're bringing us difficult art, you're a hero. Really, bless you. We need you more than we know. Shake us up. But remember that you're playing a higher-stakes game. Given our resistance to anything unfamiliar, you need an even stronger intention to reach us and make a difference in our lives. Why else should we sit through your show?

Even if the whole *point* of your play is to royally offend us, in order to accomplish your goal, you're going to need to get *in there with us*. It's easy enough to insult people in a generic way, but if you want the insult to stick, you're going to have to be specific about your target and precise in your aim.

There can be an intimacy in doing battle with the audience. If you're going to hit me, hit me where I live.

Ritual

Once you have articulated your *credo*, your higher purpose for going on stage, what do you *do* with it? Even if you feel strongly that you have the right words, it's one thing to say them, another to mean them, another to commit to them, and yet another to *re*-commit to them *every night.*

Scrawling your credo on the dressing room wall then forgetting it probably won't help. And even if you remember to look at it every day, there's certain to come a really bad day when you get to the theatre in a blue funk, and you look up at the inspiring words on the wall, and you say: yeah, *right.*

THE PRE-FLIGHT CHECKLIST: Over the years, most of the actors I know develop or evolve a set way of preparing to do a show, a routine that varies slightly in its particulars depending on the demands of the particular production, but, in the main, does not change. In part, the pre-show routine must be designed to function much like the pilot's safety checklist. Are the props where they should be? Is the voice in working order? Are the muscles sufficiently limber to prevent injury? And so on.

But there's another aspect to the routine of getting ready—and here's where you get to turn your intrinsic actor's obsessive-compulsive superstitiousness to your advantage. Theatre itself is a ritual, a secular mystery born of religious sacraments. The actor's pre-show ritual, as it has been handed down to you, serves as much to ward off bad juju (and call on the muses for inspiration) as it does to double check that the gun is in the desk drawer and the false mustache won't go flying off. Even if you know nothing about the original religious festivals that gave rise to it, you have inherited theatre's spooky side. There's a ghost in the attic; better make friends with it. Even the most hard-headed, down-to-earth, downright macho actor has some little private rite he performs or some lucky charm he keeps by the mirror to keep the boogeyman at bay.

So why not design your routine so that, in the process of readying yourself to go on stage each night, you don't *just* warm up the pipes, and you don't just make a few furtive gestures to appease the gods: you make each step a ritual to dedicate yourself to serving your audience? This seems to me so commonsensical that I would think it scarcely worth mentioning if I hadn't seen so many actors regularly put themselves through rather mechanical pre-show routines that aren't particularly thoughtful—or dependable.

WHEN DOES THE RITUAL START? On my ideal day before an evening performance, the ritual starts first thing in the morning. I wake up after eight or nine hours of sleep, eat lightly and well, exercise and do only mildly challenging tasks. In the late afternoon, after a nap, I stretch and settle in to meditate. In meditation, I first try to clear my mind, focusing on the breath, then let thoughts about the show and tonight's audience come to me slowly. . . .

Oh, I forgot: I have a job. And a four-year-old.

In real life, on the days when I have a show to do (or classes to teach— it feels very much the same to me), I *try* not to do any unnecessary or stressful things beforehand if I can avoid them. In a way, I do start the ritual first thing; I'm always aware of the show and everything I do (or don't do) is in some sense a part of preparing for it. In general, I'm as good to myself and my body as circumstances will permit.

Notice that my ideal pre-show day involves only the most minimal amounts of well-chosen food and human contact, both of which I find nourishing in moderate portions but debilitating in excess. I'm afraid that, as curtain time nears, if people try to engage me in any meaningful way— especially for someone who purports to stand for creativity, expression and close, fulfilling relationships—I can be something of a cold fish.

What feeds you well without slowing you down? If you grew up in a more frenetic environment than I'm accustomed to, you may very well find that working, chatting, playing, even arguing with people all day long leaves you feeling relaxed, rested and ready to take on playing Hamlet. It may even be the case that having your life in complete chaos gives you the energy to take on the most demanding of roles (I doubt it, but, hey, you know best). Indeed, were I a more evolved human being, I don't think I would need to husband my energies so carefully, nor would I need to be so fiercely protective of the two hours before I arrive at the theatre. But I recognize my limitations: if I'm going to give everything I've got tonight, I've got to carve out as much time as I can beforehand to relax, focus and prepare. I need solitude. Decide what you need, and try to get it. If you're not getting enough, try for more.

Think of what you're about to do as a major physical endeavor, maybe not a marathon, but at least a 10K run, maybe even a 10K *race*. You have an extraordinarily demanding job, and you may have to do it as many as six or even eight times a week, plus your day job, plus your family. You need care and feeding. Indeed, it's your professional *responsibility* to make sure you are properly nourished. Many people (probably you yourself most of all) may try to make you feel guilty for being self-centered. Be kind to them, and when it's called for apologize: of course they deserve more attention from you. But you're also going to have to be firm: this is just how it is—for now, everything goes into the show.

CLEARING: You've had a fight with your boyfriend, a terrible audition and people at work seem to have gone out of their way to make the rest of your day unpleasant. Traffic's bad, and you arrive at the theatre ten minutes late for your call (for which the stage manager justifiably gives you grief and makes you promise it will never happen again). In short, you feel like something the cat sicked up, and now, boys and girls, it's time for *Peter Pan*.

Even on a relatively good day, and with plenty of time to spare before curtain, it's a good idea to treat your arrival at the theatre as a time of transition and re-orientation. As you did in rehearsal, I'd recommend that you change your clothes first thing, not into your costume (that comes later) but into comfortable clothes best suited to your physical and vocal warmup. With a mind to shucking off the tensions you've carried in with you, you strip of your street clothes and put on your play clothes. Now: how to go about checking the rest of your baggage? If you can set it up, try this:

Exercise: Check Your Baggage.

Find someone else in the cast or crew who is like-minded and with whom you feel comfortable, set up a time to meet just before call, find a private space, sit facing each other, and spend at least five minutes each just blurting out (uninterrupted: you take the first five, then she takes the second) what's happening for you. You might want to tell her a few details of your day, but avoid epic stories. Go for what's most immediate, what is most full of feeling. Start with a physical sensation and an emotion: "I've got a crick in my neck and I'm feeling a little blue." From then on, you don't have to be coherent; it's not important whether the listener understands you or not. Indeed, as in the **Inner Monologues** *exercise from chapter 3, this one works just as well, if not better, in gibberish. Keep scanning for feelings, and when in doubt, return to the one you mentioned at the beginning. The listener's job is to look the speaker in the eye, mimic her body language, and if necessary, give the slightest prompt: "So, you're angry," or just "What else happened?"*

When you've each had a turn, take turns again, this time for two minutes each, to talk about what was happening for you while the other person was talking. Sometimes the listener is able to connect more deeply with the emotional content of the speaker's words than the speaker herself.

The times I've listed here really are the minimum. I'd recommend you allow more time. Twenty minutes apiece (with five minutes each for follow-up) is nice. If you've had a rough day (or an extraordinarily good one—you can use the time to celebrate just as well as to grumble),

twenty minutes can feel like just enough time to scratch the surface.
Further, even when you've had an unremarkable day, and you don't
think there's a lot happening for you emotionally, sometimes if you keep
on talking after you feel like you've run out of things to say, you will dis-
cover that some things are going on under the surface that you weren't
even aware of.

Of course (unless you stick to gibberish), this exercise won't be
very helpful unless you and your partner agree that you will not repeat
anything *the other says to* ***anyone***: *not to best friends, not to sisters,*
not to spouses. Be explicit about it. You need to feel safe with each
other. Even if you trust one another, it's difficult to be truthful about
what's going on in our lives without having some guarantee of
confidentiality.

⚊⚌⚊

Even if it's not practical to do this exercise with someone else on a regular basis, you can get a lot out of just asking yourself, before you start your
pre-flight checklist, what part of your personality happens to be sitting in
the captain's seat at this moment. Take a few minutes and check in with
yourself. The question of whether you're going to have an *on* night or an *off*
night tonight depends on who's piloting this plane. If it's not your higher
self, it's someone else, someone who is nowhere near qualified for the job.

If you can figure out its real name, it may be easier to coax its grubby
little hands off the controls.

THE USUAL SUSPECTS: So who's there? It helps to have in mind a file
of the people you become when you aren't at your best, a.k.a., your lower
selves. The last time you had an *off* night, who were you being?

Or project forward. You have some notion of how, when you are sub-
jected to intense pressure, you behave well and how you don't. Left to its
own self-destructive devices, how will your unconscious lead you into the
basement? In the face of your fear that the audience has turned on you, what
unproductive defensive positions are you likely to take? Will you become a

cynic, trying to pretend the audience means nothing to you, the play means nothing and life is shit anyway? How about the martyr, soldiering on in splendid isolation for your art that no one in the audience can begin to appreciate? The victim tearfully enduring their scorn? Or maybe a bully cramming the show down their throats?

Then there's my favorite: faced with a crisis, I sometimes become the man with the disappearing brain. Everything slows down. I see the other actors through a haze. I might remember that I used to be smart, but now all I am is confused. And weak. And little. And maybe, I have a bit of a cold coming on too. Maybe if I just keep still an adult will notice my distress and take care of me . . . You get the idea.

I realize that speaking of these personae as "lower" and "suspect" makes them sound criminal, bestial, even diabolical. Maybe on some level they are, or would become so if they were somehow left to themselves. But when I try to visualize my own wayward selves, I always settle on images of children trying to bluff their way through adult situations. They're not low in the sense of being evil exactly. But, especially if you've ever read *Lord of the Flies*, you're pretty certain you wouldn't want to leave them without adult supervision.

If you regard each of your lower personae as a wayward child in need of loving (but firm) guidance rather than as a raging demon in need of exorcism, you'll probably have better luck orienting towards your higher self before the show starts—and re-orienting should you happen to find you're getting off track. You notice you've regressed, so you go find your inner child at the controls. You whisper gently, "Okay, honey, I have a show to do for these nice people. Back to day care." If necessary, you promise it a treat after the show. Then you get on with your job.

FRESHENING UP: How to do something over and over again *as if for the first time?* Sustaining the life of a role in performance, especially over a long run, but even if the show only lasts two weeks requires an ongoing commitment to astonishment.

As part of your performance-day ritual, before you arrive at the theatre, give some thought to what is extraordinary about your role. You don't need to take a long time over it, nor do you need to find something brand new every day. When you're driving somewhere or you're in a boring meeting at work, just scan your memory of the role and find something that strikes you afresh.

I find it also helps me to tinker. For every performance, I'll come up with at least one thing I'm going to do slightly differently from the day before. I'm not looking to complicate things (don't go gilding the lily, okay?), but to simplify if possible, to experiment with slight variations that might make a scene funnier, more elegant, efficient, effective, etc.

The point is not to *alter* the scene—indeed, the actor has a responsibility to the director and the other actors to stick to what was rehearsed. However, except for certain technical aspects, such as fight choreography, which, for safety's sake, must remain exactly the same, tonight's show *has* to be a little different from yesterday's. We aren't machines. Shows that do not change die.

The kind of shift I'm talking about may be so subtle that the other actors, even though they pick up on it unconsciously, don't even notice that anything's different. Moreover, once I get into the scene, I may even end up discarding my idea on the fly. No matter. When I've oriented to the *possibility* of playing things differently, even if I make choices almost identical to the night before, I will tend to come to them with a greater sense of freshness.

WARMING UP: I'm something of a magpie about warmups, stealing exercises from acting classes and books, choir rehearsals, sports, martial arts, yoga—actually, I scarcely know the origins anymore. I'm guessing you too probably already have at least a beginning repertoire of favorites, so I'm not going to prescribe particular exercises to you. On one level, just like the rest of the actor's pre-flight checklist, warmups are purely practical: you're making sure that you'll be able to make yourself heard and that your performance isn't hampered by unnecessary physical tension. Unless you've learned to do something that's actually painful or dangerous (if something hurts, modify it, okay?), I think it's unimportant *which* exercises you use, so long as you have the sense of dedicating *every part* of yourself to the task ahead.

Acting teachers rather grandly refer to the actor's voice and body as his *instrument.* I say, take it all the way: go ahead and think of yourself as a Stradivarius. If ever there was a time to indulge your narcissism, this is it. Warming up is also *psyching up.* Believe me, I'm a modest physical specimen, but still, when I'm doing a good, thorough theatrical warmup, I think I'm pretty slick. Whether I'm conscious of it or not, during warmups there's a voice in my head saying something to the effect of, "What a piece of work is *me.*"

Okay, maybe it's a bit delusional, but why not have your own cheering section as you get ready for the big game? It doesn't matter at all whether or not you're conventionally (or even unconventionally) attractive, whether you're in good physical condition or even whether you're particularly graceful. You can be downright homely; no matter: you're an actor; they're coming to see *you.* Never mind your shortcomings; consider your assets. As you do your vocal exercises, conjure an appreciative audience and think: "I can do *this* with my **voice**! Hark! I speak tongue twisters with clarity and precision! And listen to my *range!*" And as you stretch your limbs and put your vertebrae in their proper alignment, take a little time to marvel at the sheer *craftsmanship* that went into building you such a body. Amazing.

Okay, so you're preening. Why not? If you weren't something of a showoff, you wouldn't be doing this. But more importantly, you're getting ready to share your physical presence *with your audience.* Apologizing for your voice and body will serve no one.

RE-DIRECTING TENSION AND FEAR: God bless tension and fear— our greatest renewable human resources. Let's talk about how to put them to good use.

First, don't let anyone tell you to relax—even if you're doing what are commonly called "relaxation exercises": stretching, deep breathing, meditation, etc. While I do find the process of warming up calming, I think the actor who actually tries to *relax* before a show is courting a kind of delusion. I relax before I go to *sleep*. Before I go on stage, I'm *scared*. There's some serious voltage passing through my system. I don't see any percentage in trying to relax. Instead, I'm interested in gathering and focusing some of that power on the task at hand.

Notice what happens when you do, for example, a hamstring stretch: right afterwards, though you have more ability to remain still, you actually have more energy in your legs. That's the feeling I'm aiming for when I stretch: I want the sense that I could happily keep my hands in my lap for the next hour—*or*, if I needed to, I could put my fist through the wall. You don't want to be relaxed; you want to be *poised*. Not a jellyfish, but a panther. So when you are stretching your muscles, taking inventory of your working parts, and you find an area of tension, don't try to release it into the ether. Re-direct the energy to where it's needed: store it for the show.

Likewise with fear. On one level, what a wonderfully practical emotion. Nervous? Well, maybe there's really something to be nervous *about*. If you find yourself getting the pre-show willies, don't ignore them. There may be useful information there. If you've got a bad feeling, go re-check your props (maybe you *did* miss something the first time). Check your memory: yep, you still remember your first line; the rest of them are probably still there too. Still nervous? Good. That means you're reasonably aware of what you're about to do. Rather than just distracting yourself from this fear, or trying to conquer it or somehow dissipate it, let's put it to good use.

There's no understanding this kind of fear. You won't be able to talk yourself out of it. Yes, you say to yourself, the show will probably be fine. But your fear isn't rational. It's an animal response to a threatening situation. If your fear level is manageable, you may just want to notice it, sit with it, monitor it as you go about your routine. Really, there's not a lot of difference between the feeling of fear and that of excitement, anticipation or suspense. Remember, people regularly pay good money to have the daylights scared out of them (horror movies, roller coasters, etc.). This shot of fear is totally on the house. If you can find a way to be *thankful* for your fear, you're in good shape. Ooh, butterflies in the stomach: *nice*.

NAKED AGGRESSION: Once fear reaches a certain pitch, however, it's almost impossible to enjoy it. Sometimes, you can't just monitor the fear; you have to manage it. What's sometimes called the "animal" part of us (that is, the part of our nervous system that reacts to stimuli without the intervention of conscious thought) has three possible responses to threat: we flee, freeze or fight. Most of us have a "preferred" strategy (I tend to freeze), but we're capable of all three, and we're capable of consciously converting from one to strategy to another when our response to events isn't proving to be adaptive. (Unlike an opossum, you can see that your first impulse to freeze won't save you from the oncoming semi.) While you may not be able to alter the fact that you've come down with a bad case of stage fright, you may be able to exercise some choice as to which animal response you will follow.

Let's review your options. Run screaming from the theatre? That's probably out. And if there's anything that makes an actor's terror *worse*, it's the prospect of freezing. That leaves combat: you against the audience. Hey, you're outnumbered, but I think it's your best alternative.

Olivier suffered from a considerable and recurrent problem with stage fright. Here's one technique he used to re-channel his anxiety:

> Go to the theatre early on the first night and get made up well in advance of the curtain. Then walk on to the stage and imagine that the curtain is already up and that you are facing the audience. Look out at them and shout, "You are about to see the greatest fucking performance of your entire theatre-going lives. And I will be giving it. You lucky people."

Notice how his ritual combines rampant narcissism with naked aggression (shouting and cussing at the audience—you tell 'em, Larry). He's not just bluffing. He's ready to go out there and, as the comedians say, slay them, *knock them dead*.

Strange but true. If your level of fear is such that it might get between you and your audience, you need to be ready to fight—not the fear, but the *audience itself*. The performance is something you're going to *do to* them, whether they like it or not. Remember, they think that you can't fool them, that you can't manipulate them. Well, they've got another think coming, don't they? You're about to hit them with your best shot. The lucky people . . .

If you do channel your fear into aggression, don't lose sight of your ultimate goal. Just being a badass isn't going to help you or the audience (and neither will strutting around like a rock star) unless you're doing it in the service of a greater good.

IMAGINING THE WORST: Sometimes, instead of giving me a jolt of energy, stage fright feels like a weight pressing down on the back of my neck. In fact, the feeling is barely recognizable as fright, because it manifests as a stew of lethargy and dull resentment. My eyelids feel heavy, and there's a buzzing in my head like the sound of bad fluorescent lighting in a bus station at 3:00 AM. I page my higher self, but my higher self has left the building. As for the audience, they can go rot.

At such times, instead of trying to wrestle the controls away from the scared little punk who is flying the plane, I encourage him to go ahead and fly it smack into a cliff.

Exercise: Oops.

> *Imagine that tonight will be the **worst** fucking performance of the audience's theatre-going lives, and that it will be **all your fault**. Imagine the audience stalking out, demanding their money back. Not only do you get fired, but, in a special meeting, the membership of Actor's Equity bans you for life—even if you never joined. Then flash forward: at the end of your long life, you are working as a "greeter" in a fast food place. On your breaks, you annoy your co-workers with stories about how you used to be on the stage.*

*Better yet, tell the whole story of your imminent spectacular fail-
ure to another actor. (Choose someone stable with a sense of humor.)
The more dramatic, the more exaggerated you make it, the better.
Then quit the drama and, in the manner of a gleeful two-year-old
dropping food on the floor, say, "So there goes my life. Oops."*

⸻⁓⸻

While the actors I know are (mostly) sensible people, they do tend to be
a wee bit dramatic about their own lives. Sometimes, if you just dive into the
fear, you come up feeling refreshed. So contemplate the mayhem, the damage, the pain you are about to cause yourself and others. Then say, "Oops,
soorree." Usually, this will be enough to get you to lighten up.

Fear tends to isolate us, so telling your sensational tale to another actor
is also a good reminder that you're not alone—nor would you be alone in
trying to get a faltering show back on track. I once heard a story about an
actor whose character gets killed early on in the play. On opening night, as
soon as he stepped on stage the actor realized he couldn't remember any of
his lines, so he just dropped dead. The other actors improvised around him
and, when the time came, carried him off stage.

While it's probably apocryphal, I take great comfort from this story. I tell
myself that if I ever reach the point where everything's gone wrong, I'm paralyzed with fear and I can't think of anything to say or do about it, I'll just do
a little death scene and let the other actors figure it out. In fact, when we're
doing improvisations in my acting classes, I always give actors the option of
dropping dead. When an actor's mind goes blank, he clutches his chest and
sinks to the floor. The class shouts, "Actor down!" Two actors run on stage
and carry off the corpse of their fallen comrade, and another brave actor
takes up the improvisation.

My goal in class is that the actors learn to anticipate and even court dis-
aster. Instead of cringing at the possibility of a debacle, far better to adopt
the manner of a pugnacious street drunk and slur, "Bring it on." I once saw
a student production in which one of the lead actors was an alcoholic.

It was a memory play, skipping around in time, flashing back and flashing forward. The problem wasn't exactly that the actor in question forgot his lines; it was that he never did them in the same order twice. Thus, the rest of the cast never knew which scene was coming when. Obviously, it wasn't an ideal state of affairs, and the play didn't always make a lot of sense, but I tell you that show was *live*. Those actors were *concentrating*.

Mind you, I'm not recommending you work with undependable addicts just for the thrill of it. Nor should you allow yourself to become lax in your preparations just because a touch of danger sharpens the senses. If anything, you should over-prepare. But, at the same time, I find it helps to tempt the fates to throw you a curveball or two. Mishap—like first night jitters—can be a friend to the actor's double consciousness.

One time, in the middle of the third act of a farce, the actor opposite me abruptly started spouting dialogue from act one. Suddenly, I couldn't remember where we had been in act three. I answered his mis-cue with my own line from act one. So we kept on, both lost in a spontaneous reprise of act one. Of course it was terrifying, but it was also kind of cool. Believe me: if you haven't tried to *simultaneously* play a scene and figure out how to find your way out of a screwup like that, you haven't *lived*. Eventually, we got back on track and continued the show. Except for a slight touch of déjà vu, I don't think anyone in the audience noticed. And from then on our performance of act three was the best we did in the whole run.

RALLYING THE TROOPS: Surely you've done this before: you're going out for the evening, maybe to a party or on a date. In order to get things rolling you put a particular song on the stereo. Why not do that as part of your warmup? If certain music gets you going (no matter whether it's Sousa marches or Bach Cantatas or Eminem), bring your Discman. Maybe go find a place to play some air guitar.

Music's an obvious choice, but you may want to consider priming the pump with other media: poems, film clips, paintings, etc. What inspires you? What fills you with fire? I like to read aloud Henry V's "band of brothers" speech. Look it up. Talk about coming from a higher self—outnumbered ten to one, here is a man who is (or at least seems to be) ready, *eager* to die for his beliefs. In the face of almost certain defeat, instead of threatening or talking down to his men, he elevates them, makes them all warrior kings. And here's the thing: this guy's spent most of his life in taverns, not on the battlefield—in the best sense of the word, he's *acting*.

What will rally *your* troops? Keep some art on hand.

TRANSFORMATION: I dislike chatter in the dressing room—which I believe tends to stem from nervous tension rather than any real desire to socialize. When I'm putting on my costume and makeup, I want to concentrate. There's something happening in that mirror and inside me.

Don't underestimate the profound effect of altering your appearance. As a society, when we want to endow ordinary people with authority, in a solemn ceremony, we in*vest* them. The robe of office is meant to be not just a costume, not just a symbol; it is a *manifestation* of the wise use of power. The priest's vestments, the judge's robes, the policeman's uniform are intended to transform the wearer into someone not just with uncommon power but with uncommon purity of heart. Would that the ritual always worked.

To some extent, I suppose, I'm "getting into character;" at least in the sense of reminding myself what the person I'm playing looks like. But my experience is that the character in me only really comes to life on stage under the special circumstances of the play itself. So sitting around pre-show trying to "be" the person I'm going to play seems to me a great waste of mental effort, and in some actors, left unchecked, it becomes an annoying affectation. The actor who, because he's playing Puck, runs around back stage speaking in doggerel and playing little tricks on people isn't "getting into character"; he's just pissing everyone off. If you want to start speaking in your dialect or practicing your facial tics, that's great; I'm with you. But the show starts on stage. Please, no head games.

To me, the investment that happens when I put on a costume is less about getting into character than it is about assuming the mantle of the actor. As I put on makeup, I come to realize in a more profound way, that I'm about to play someone else. The people coming to see the show are entrusting me with a responsibility that I don't take lightly. I want to bring them something that's honest, fresh, lively. The more seriously I take this part of the ritual, the more joyful and excited I feel. I don't just want to do well, I want to do good.

Exercise: Extending Your Reach.

During the meditation or prayer part of your routine (see below), take a few moments to concentrate on your breath.

Then, with each breath in imagine that you are taking warmth, light, energy into your body. With each breath out, imagine yourself radiating that energy to the other actors and the audience.

*Now, dedicate tonight's performance to the people in the audience who are in the **worst** shape to appreciate it. Some of us are in pain, worried, benighted. We need you. Extend yourself. Be a beacon to us.*

—◦◦◦—

PRAYER: When I'm directing, if circumstances permit, I try to work a group prayer into the pre-show ritual, but I almost never *call it* a prayer. In a sense, all I'm asking of the cast is to take a moment to wish the audience well and to wish ourselves well. In thinking about what we're about to do, why not project our best intentions out into the world? Why not come together and ask to be of service? You can ask Jesus or Allah or Buddha if you like, but you can also just ask your higher self to come out and play. In my experience, it doesn't matter at all what you believe or disbelieve in; prayer is an effective technique and a necessary counterbalance to the actor's healthy (and sometimes not-so-healthy) ego. (Oddly enough, I think Olivier's blustering pre-show monologue is a kind of prayer. He is using a ritual incantation to summon his own powers, but he's clearly doing so for the benefit of his audience and his art.)

Here's how I work it: just before it's time to clear the house, the actors gather for a few minutes to do a brief, energetic shared warmup, something boisterous that will give everyone a collective sense of completion about their individual warmups. Then, the crew joins us, and we form a cluster, everyone standing very close, everyone with a hand on someone else's shoulder or back. Often, it's enough for people to just remain there silently for a moment, everyone paying attention to the moment, the reality of being together, and the breath. Sometimes I'll remind everyone of why I believe the show is important, why the audience needs us, what my wishes are for them (and for us), and I'll ask everyone to remember their own wishes for the audience. Then, quietly, we all head off to do our jobs.

Simple as that. But I've found that it's usually enough to get the cast and crew aligned and focused. If we stick to the ritual, the show will have few, if any, off nights, and will steadily improve throughout the run. If we neglect it, it's anyone's guess whether tonight's show will be worth watching. To my mind, every part of the pre-show ritual is a prayer, but this ending part—especially if the whole cast and crew can do it together—is the most powerful act of devotion.

Every night: think what you stand for. Think well of yourself. Think well of your audience. Remember your spine. Remember your first line. Launch.

CHAPTER 8

Afterwards: What Actors Learn

EAT RIGHT, GET PLENTY OF REST AND DRINK LOTS OF WATER. Buckle your seatbelt. Floss.

Really: I mean it. During the run of a show, you need to think seriously—more seriously than usual—about taking care of yourself. It's not just that other people are depending on you: it's that you have somehow to come to terms with the day-in and day-out intensity of performing.

CURTAIN CALLS AND COMPLIMENTS: Accepting applause gracefully is a skill worth cultivating. You need to figure out how to let it in and enjoy it. We in the audience are sending you a message of appreciation; we like to know that you're receiving it. That's not to say you should *milk* the moment; indeed, if you have any say about the length or complexity of the curtain call, do your part to keep it short and sweet. (A simple gesture towards the booth, acknowledging the tech crew, is also a nice touch.) But do let us know that you see and hear us clapping and hollering. Why be stiff? You enjoy your job, right? Admit it: that was *fun*.

People will compliment you after the show. Some will be sincere and some may not. Some will be accurate, and some may not. No matter. Just say thank you. *Never* disagree with a compliment. It demeans you, the show, your art, and the giver of the compliment.

For some people, receiving praise for a job well done can be much more stressful than taking blame for a fiasco. A lot of actors are remarkably private people. However much they may thrive on the attention they receive when they are on stage, they have a harder time accepting it one-on-one afterwards. It's embarrassing. It's so *personal*.

Or maybe you just can't get enough of curtain calls and compliments (wouldn't it be nice if *everyone* got an extended round of applause from 500 people at the end of the workday?). No matter. Either way, you need to recognize that you've just been given a stimulant, like a shot of espresso at 10:30 PM. Now what? Sleep can be a problem, and, in the long run, so can burn-out. Developing or deepening a dependence on alcohol and drugs is also a real threat. You need a positive plan to maintain your physical and mental health, both for your own sake and for the sakes of your family and friends.

COOL DOWN: You need a buffer, and a healthy one, between stage life and ordinary life. This is especially true if you are playing an emotionally demanding role, but I think it's a mistake to underestimate the effects of performing less demanding parts. You've been in front of an audience. I don't care how easy the role is for you or how many times you've done it; it's a big deal.

Athletes structure a cool-down period into their exercise regimes. Do you have one? Early in the day, certainly *before* the show rather than after it, think about how you're going to come down. What will the rest of your evening look like after the curtain comes down? What will you do? Where will you go? Who will you talk to? What will you eat and drink? When will you go to bed?

Do I sound like your mom? Well, okay, I'll stop.

The point is: in all likelihood, you'll need calming, so give yourself a conscious exit strategy, whatever that looks like for you. Otherwise your exit strategy will be *un*conscious—and you know what that means: you're headed for that basement. I've seen people use the stress of performance to justify all kinds of destructive behavior. You don't have to stick to every detail of your plan, but be sure you *have* one.

Feedback

DEBRIEFING: Your post-show plan should probably include talking through the show—if only to blow off steam. You can try doing this with the other actors, but you may find that you get more out of it if you set aside some time to be with a good listener who *isn't* directly involved with the show. Even if you only take a few minutes to review the evening, to celebrate what went well and pick apart what didn't go so well, it may help you wind down. Don't underestimate the value of 20–20 hindsight. Obviously, talking can be therapeutic, but more importantly, debriefing is essential to growing in the part: by talking through what you did and how it worked, you solidify your gains and set your sights on what you want to improve. By the end of the session, you'll probably have a good idea what you'd like to tinker with in tomorrow's show.

Be as truthful as you can, and be kind to yourself. We all know what it's like to be your own worst critic. Set your sights on being your own *best* critic.

CRITICISM: Now that the show is set and in front of an audience, for better or worse, at this point, you're committed to certain parameters in playing the role. You need to think carefully about what kind of feedback you're going to get, when you're going to get it, and from whom.

After a show has finished previews, I stop giving actors notes. If asked, I will give an actor feedback after a performance, but even then, I try to ask a lot of questions rather than doling out opinions. When I do offer guidance, it tends to be strategic rather than tactical. Though, if the actor asks me about a particular moment (or I see an easy instant fix for a technical problem), I might say something about it, usually, I'll confine any comments to the broader aspects of her performance: pacing, structure, etc. If a scene has lost something, I might remind her of key things we've already worked on, but I'll steer clear of introducing any new ideas. She's got enough to think about.

I figure: the actor is the one up on the tightrope, not me. If I'm down below shouting, "Lean left! No, lean right!" how useful is that likely to be?

Truly constructive criticism can be a lifeline for the actor; it helps you grow both in the role and in your craft. However, even when you solicit opinions from people you trust, you're going to have to sort out for yourself whether the notes you're getting are likely to benefit you or knock you off balance. To that end, it may help for you to formulate specific questions rather than just taking potluck in people's reactions. Tell them what you're *trying* to do, and ask them if they think it's coming across.

Until the show closes, if someone tells you that you need to change anything fundamental in your approach to the part, it's probably best to treat their suggestion (however well-intentioned it might be) as you would a suspicious package in a train station. Leave it alone. Remain calm. Walk away. And call the authorities if you're worried: the director, for example. She may be able to help you sort out what's useful from what's not—and to safely dispose of anything destructive.

NEWSPAPERS: If you know your show is going to be reviewed, think hard about whether you want to read what the critics have to say, especially if it's negative. A little self-assessment is in order: How good are you at not taking things personally? How quickly do you get up again when someone knocks you flat? If you're a sensitive soul, own it without apology. Set up a defensive perimeter. Shield yourself from random criticism, and ask the people around you to help.

But if you're a fairly confident, steady person, it may be that reading a bad review won't unsettle you much. Indeed, some actors can take even the most unhelpful, hateful or obscure review, extract whatever useful information it may contain, and discard the rest (though they may go off by themselves and sob a little bit first). If you're confident in your work, somebody not liking you is just one more piece of data—a phenomenon you might want to investigate rather then an indictment of your talent. Again, if need be, go check it out with your director; ask if she thinks the reviewer has a point. You're not going to make major changes, but maybe some small adjustment is in order.

USING A MENTOR: If you haven't yet found a mentor, you'd do well to be on the lookout. Set a high standard. Obviously, he should be someone whose work you admire and whose opinion you trust, but those aren't the only qualifications. It helps if he not only has seen your work but has worked with you enough to get a sense of who you are as an actor and as a person. A good mentor will always tell you the truth without coddling you, flattering you or hedging. But being a mentor doesn't just involve giving advice, it means giving the right advice *for you* at the right moment in your development. A mentor isn't just interested in sharing his expertise; he is committed to your professional and personal well-being. So when you believe you have found someone who is capable of helping in this way, *ask*.

And be aware that you are taking on a set of responsibilities as well—among them: to use his time well, to take his coaching in good faith rather than becoming defensive, and, if you find his authority imposing, to remember that he is a colleague and a human being. When you get to the point where you rebel against his advice, resolve to do so openly, consciously and with your sense of humor intact. Above all, don't run off because you don't think you can face his disapproval. Stick around. With any luck, you'll *both* learn something.

Strike

One advantage of community or college theatre is that everyone involved with the show participates in tearing down the set and packing away the costumes. The physical act of dismantling the show is one of my favorite theatrical rituals. Without it, I believe I would have a harder time managing the transition back to life-as-usual. I think of strike as a midnight festival, something akin to an Irish wake, but instead of getting drunk, we all get to use power tools (please don't do *both*).

In its evanescence, theatre is a rehearsal for dying. We work hard—and joyously—and yet very little remains afterward. We inhabit a whole life, and we move on. We fall in love with people, then say good-bye.

Take some time during strike to let that sink in. Notice how little time it is taking to strip the stage down to bare walls. Notice how conversations trail off. Some people are giddy. Others are grim. They may not realize it yet, but they are grieving.

There's no need to be somber, but if you're sad, why deny it? Just *mentioning* sadness to the people working next to you can bring about a shared release of tension. And then people begin to work together more efficiently and joyfully. Soon what was a chore turns into a *celebration* of the part of your life that is passing on. In New Orleans, they play Dixieland at funerals. If you're in a professional situation where actors are not part of the strike, bring the same mindfulness to the closing night party. Bring some healthy food to share. Celebrate, but keep conscious.

REST: It used to be that after every show, I would come down with a cold. Sometimes I'd feel the first tickle at the back of my throat before strike was over. Lately, I've learned to plan for a couple of "down" days after a show closes. This seems to pre-empt my body's tendency to shut me down against my will. I try to keep work to a bare minimum and spend as much time as I can doing nothing at all. I'd much rather just skip this enforced rest period and get busy again.

I'd much rather play. But, I remind myself gently but firmly, it's nap time.

Post-Mortem

When your mentor comes to see the show, you might want to ask him to hold his comments until a couple of weeks after closing. That way, he'll be able to tell you what he thinks without worrying about interfering with your performance. And you may be in a more receptive frame of mind. In my experience, during a show, or right after it closes, I'm far too invested in the experience to consider my work objectively. After a fortnight, I'm more ready to *learn* from my mistakes and successes.

If you know other members of your cast who are seriously interested in self-assessment, you might also consider setting up a time to meet and do a post-mortem on the show. Start out by talking about the positive parts of the group's process: celebrate the parts of your collaboration that you really enjoyed; compliment people who made everyone's experience of rehearsal more joyous (be specific: detailed compliments to individuals are much more valuable than generalized "aw-you-guys-are-great" compliments). Then spend some time discussing what parts of the group's process didn't go as well as you would have liked—hardships and blind alleys in rehearsal, miscommunications, etc.—and talk about how things could have been improved.

If the group is emotionally skilled enough, this would be the time for anyone who finds he is carrying some hurt or resentment towards someone else in the group to express it directly and responsibly. The point is not to shame or lash out at the other person, but rather to make sure that any future working relationship between the two of you is free of undeclared baggage. Keep a cool head until you can clear up any misunderstandings. If you find you've hurt someone, apologize. If everyone agrees to keep things simple, civil and contained, you should come out the other side of this part with a feeling of closeness and a heightened ability to give one another feedback that is both honest and compassionate.

Exercise: Fly on the Wall.

*One member of the group turns her back on the group, and everyone talks about her and her work as if she weren't in the room. What are her strengths and weaknesses as a performer? How do people in the group prize working with her? When do they find her difficult? What do they wish she would do more of? Finally, and most importantly: What do people in the group wish **for** her?*

When the group is done, the "absent" member rejoins the group and takes a few minutes to respond.

In my theatre department, after every show, we do a post-mortem gathering of actors, stage managers, and director, and we generally follow the format just described. I act as facilitator, and how far we go depends on both my assessment of the group's emotional maturity and the students' willingness and interest in self-evaluation. The *Fly on the Wall* exercise is strictly for volunteers; no one should ever be compelled to do it. Nor should the group attempt it unless there really is a general sense that no one is harboring any unresolved grudges.

I should add though, that, without exception, every actor who has volunteered for the exercise has not only learned a great deal but has been moved (often deeply) by the experience. It's not just that the volunteer receives plenty of compliments and good wishes. Actually, sometimes the group's *criticism* of the volunteer feels even better.

However hard we may try to disguise our failings, it often comes as an unexpected relief to find that they are nonetheless in full view and obvious to everyone. At the deepest level—for all the roles we play—we are desperate for other people to *see* us as we really are.

What Actors Learn

Some people find surgeons creepy. Surgeons cut people. But, except in certain notable horror flicks, they try to use that power to the good. And while they may wield sharp things in the operating room, they don't take that part of their work home with them.

A lot of people also mistrust actors. You know how to lie. Not only that, you know how to find the drama in any situation and increase it. But ability, and the power that comes with it, are neutral. How will you put your abilities to use? That's the question.

There's something to be said for keeping a firewall between your stage life and your personal life. You don't want to go around fooling people and creating dramatic situations just for the thrill, okay? If you do, please get help (and for God's sake, stay out of politics). Continuing stage relationships into real life is also a dicey business. For example, though I'm sure there are exceptions, playing a love scene with someone usually isn't a good basis for beginning an offstage romantic relationship. It's not that what you're feeling for the other person isn't real, but that it's based on fictional circumstances.

The ability to do something unusually well often brings with it an extraordinary competence in doing the opposite. Many muscular, physically imposing people learn to move with great delicacy and to treat others with surprising gentleness. And the surgeon's job is ultimately not about creating wounds but about healing them. Your skill in escalating drama means that you are also capable of recognizing and *de-escalating* it. The ability to consciously deceive yourself and others carries with it a corresponding ability, indeed an obligation, to live more truthfully.

This is the part of the work you *should* be taking home with you.

ACTORS LEARN TO CREATE INTENTIONAL RELATIONSHIPS WITH OTHER PEOPLE. As you learn your trade, you become expert in crafting relationships on stage. Why *wouldn't* you apply your skills to deepen your friendships, strengthen your professional ties, and create more loving, fulfilling relationships with your family?

ACTORS LEARN THAT LOVE CAN BE A DELIBERATE ACT, NOT JUST SOMETHING THAT HAPPENS TO US. If you can play love scenes with relative strangers, imagine what you can accomplish with your strange relatives.

ACTORS LEARN TO SWITCH ROLES. Having had some experience *deliberately* creating dysfunctional relationships, you have an enhanced ability to recognize when you have done so *unconsciously* and to shift to higher ground.

ACTORS LEARN ABOUT THE USES AND ABUSES OF SOCIAL STATUS. Oppression and victimhood aren't just global political phenomena, but daily personal experiences. Actors learn to perceive and correct for the quotidian violence we do to one another and to ourselves.

ACTORS LEARN TO IDENTIFY AND PURSUE WHAT THEY WANT: Not just your surface wants but your deeper longings.

ACTORS LEARN THAT THE SELF IS A CONSTRUCT AND, AS SUCH, IS NOT FIXED FOREVER. Such flexibility is required of the actor that she comes to recognize that what most of us think of as a "self" is chiefly a set of limitations imposed by past experience. Even those parts of the self that come to us through heredity or culture are only pre-dispositions, not immutable laws. The actor learns that her own temperament is not her destiny. With sufficient concentration, practice and will, we can change our*selves*, and that means, if we choose to, we can change for the better.

ACTORS LEARN THAT LIFE IS FUNNY. The actor learns to take on the character's struggles with great seriousness even as she plays them for laughs. At your best, you are in the world, but not of it. In the bleakest situations, humor saves us. Of course, laughter relieves tension, but beyond more than that, keeping a sense of ironic detachment can allow us to keep our pain in perspective. As Wavy Gravy famously said, "If you haven't got a sense of humor, it just isn't funny."

ACTORS LEARN THAT THEY ARE ORDINARY PEOPLE. Acting tends to be humbling, and not just because it is difficult. Characters are flawed; in part, that's what makes them interesting. Even Superman has his kryptonite; without it, he would be a muscle-bound bore. For an actor, every failure to recognize the faults of others in himself is a missed opportunity. In order to be successful, the actor has to undergo a daily process of noticing, accepting and, when it's called for, exploiting and exposing his own character flaws. While they may be adept at self-promotion, actors come to realize that there is also considerable power in self-deprecation.

ACTORS LEARN TO MAKE THEMSELVES VULNERABLE. In a hostile world, toughness is commonplace. Actors learn to show us what's underneath.

ACTORS LEARN TO FAIL. Some perfectionists actually boast about their condition as if it were a virtue rather than a crippling disease. In its most extreme form, perfectionism means keeping one's work secret until it is flawless—which, more often than not, means keeping it secret *for good*. Actors cannot afford to be perfectionists. In rehearsal, you have to fail repeatedly, publicly, extravagantly, and without unnecessary apology.

ACTORS LEARN THE RELATIONSHIP BETWEEN PLANNING AND SPONTANEITY. In your best performances, you act and react to the rest of the cast and the audience in the moment. But spontaneity like that doesn't just *happen*. You know how much advance preparation it takes to be *truly* spontaneous.

ACTORS LEARN TO SERVE THE ENTERPRISE RATHER THAN THE EGO. Acting teaches us that any time we're lost, we need to turn to other people to find our way. It's not just that theatre is an intensely collaborative medium. Even a "star vehicle," even a one-man show is not about the actor but about the audience. The moment the actor forgets that, he is cast adrift.

ACTORS LEARN TO PLAY. Sometimes, adults forget how. Or they confuse the concepts of play and pleasure. Actors (and athletes) know that, while playing hard is not always exactly pleasurable, when all is said and done it's the only game in town.

ACTORS LEARN TO RECOGNIZE WHEN THEY ARE FULL OF SHIT. You know what it's like. The breathing is all wrong. The hands fly about like startled pigeons. The feet wander. So, stop. Level with yourself. Then you can level with others.

ACTORS LEARN TO TALK TO, NOT AT, PEOPLE. See above.

ACTORS LEARN TO LISTEN TO THE BODY. It thinks faster than your brain. Sometimes, it's more accurate.

ACTORS LEARN THAT THE BODY IS A VEHICLE. When you're on stage, you could be anyone. Wear a fat suit, and you're fat. Stand in a lavender spotlight, and you'll have beautiful skin. Play a part where all the men are after your body, and you're attractive. When you've grown accustomed to driving so *many* vehicles in this life, does it really matter which one you happen to own?

ACTORS LEARN TO INCORPORATE FEELING AND THINKING. Clarity about emotions is inseparable from clear thinking and perception. We cannot know what we think without knowing what we feel. You have the good fortune to pursue a trade that puts great stock in the ability to recognize and express emotions. You have practice in following gut feelings. As such, we need you around when we're making important decisions. When we're headed off the rails, when something's wrong, even if you can't say why, you may be the first one in the room to feel angry or disgusted. When something's missing, you may be the first to sense its absence. But you're not just the canary in the coal mine: you can also be the wolf scenting the wind. When an opportunity arises, you may be the first to recognize it.

ACTORS LEARN TO EXPRESS EMOTION. What a fine, generous thing: filling a room, an *amphitheatre* with emotion. People are starving for it, including your friends, your family, your co-workers. When you break our taboos, our strictures against expression, you both free us and feed us. And you model how we might feed ourselves.

ACTORS LEARN TO CONTAIN IT. Containment is not the same thing as shutting down. The performer learns to feel things strongly, but to choose wisely the time and place to express them.

ACTORS LEARN NOT TO FETISHIZE EMOTION. To people unaccustomed to recognizing, expressing, and handling emotion, when strong feelings do arise, they are often accompanied by a sense of crisis. Actors learn that, like thoughts or sensations, even the most powerful emotions are fleeting. It's a paradox: anger, fear, pain, sadness, love—they are vital to us. They're also no big deal.

ACTORS LEARN TO INTERRUPT IT. Like an audio system amplifying and re-amplifying its own noise, there is a point where our emotional response, if left unchecked, can spin out of control. Temper tantrums are the obvious example. As an actor, being accustomed to making emotional distinctions, you are better able to recognize that moment in the argument when your anger has turned into ranting and bullying. You stop, breathe, change your approach. Similarly, you know when your fear is starting to transform to hysteria, when your sadness verges on self-pity, and so on. In other words, when it comes to emotion, you don't just know how to turn up the volume: you can also change the channel.

ACTORS LEARN TO LOOK DEEPER. Under every emotion is another emotion. Behind every impulse, there's a deeper desire. Actors aren't satisfied with just looking at the pretty rocks on the seashore; they want to see the life that's under them.

ACTORS LEARN TO PERSONALIZE. Sometimes it can be very hard for us to care about other people, but that's the actor's *job*. As an actor, you have to find a way to make the character's concerns your concerns. It's not just a matter of generalized empathy: you learn to find the details that will compel you to feel as the character feels, behave as the character behaves. In this regard, acting is an antidote to de-personalization. It is anti-racist. It is anti-violent. It is anti-war.

ACTORS LEARN TO HAVE FAITH. Sometimes belief, like grace, is easy: it simply arrives, a perfect gift. But faith, the *resolve* to believe even when belief is difficult, takes practice. The actor resolves to believe in the goodness of the play, the character and ultimately the audience.

ACTORS LEARN THE POWER OF METAPHOR AND ANALOGY. Art is how we learn to live our lives. An apt metaphor is a sacrament; it transforms how we perceive the world and so transforms *us*. Make no mistake; this is your calling: every time you step onto a stage, remember what you *stand for*.

Bibliography

Adler, Stella, and Kissel, Howard. *Stella Adler on the Art of Acting*. New York: Applause Theatre Book Publishers, 2000.

Adler, Stella. *The Technique of Acting*. New York: Bantam Books, 1978.

Ahart, John. *The Director's Eye: a Comprehensive Textbook for Directors and Actors*. Colorado Springs, CO: Meriwether Pub., 2001.

Allen, David. *Stanislavski for Beginners*. New York: Writers and Readers Press, 1999.

Ball, William. *A Sense of Direction*. New York: Drama Publishers, 1984.

Barton, John. *Playing Shakespeare*. London and New York: Methuen, 1984.

Barton, Robert. *Acting on Stage and Off*, 3rd ed. Belmont, CA: Wadsworth, 2002.

Benedetti, Robert. *The Actor at Work*, 8th ed. Boston: Allyn and Bacon, 2001.

Benedetti, Robert. *The Actor in You*, 2nd ed. New York: Pearson, 2003.

Berry, Cicely. *The Actor and the Text*. New York: Applause Theatre Book Publishers, 1992.

Bild, Kathryn Marie. *Acting from a Spiritual Perspective*. Hanover, NH: Smith & Kraus, 2002.

Boal, Augusto. *Games for Actors and Non-Actors*, trans. Adrian Jackson. London and New York: Routledge, 1992.

Boal, Augusto. *Theatre of the Oppressed*, trans. Charles A. & Maria-Odilia Leal McBride. New York: Theatre Communications Group, 1995.

Boleslavski, Richard. *Acting: The First Six Lessons*. New York: Theatre Arts Books, 1933.

Brestoff, Richard. U*nder the Circumstances: Variations on a Theme of Stanislavski: A Step by Step Approach to Playing a Part*. Hanover, NH: Smith & Kraus, 1999.

Bruder, Melissa, et al. *A Practical Handbook for the Actor*. New York: Vintage, 1986.

Callow, Simon. *Being an Actor*. New York: Picador, 1984.

Carlson, Marvin. *Theories of the Theatre*. Ithaca, NY, and London: Cornell University Press, 1984.

Chaikin, Joseph. *The Presence of the Actor.* New York: Atheneum, 1972.

Chekhov, Michael. *To the Actor: On the Technique of Acting.* New York: Routledge, 2002.

Clurman, Harold. *On Directing.* New York: Fireside Book, 1997.

Cohen, Robert. *Acting One,* 4th ed. Columbus, OH: McGraw-Hill, 2002.

Cole, Toby and Chinoy, Helen Krich, eds. *Actors on Acting.* New York: Crown Publishers, 1949.

Csikszentmihalyi, Mihaly. *Flow: The Psychology of Optimal Experience.* New York: Harper Perennial, 1991.

Damasio, Antonio. *Descartes' Error: Emotion, Reason and the Human Brain.* New York: G.P. Putnam, 1994.

Damasio, Antonio. *Looking for Spinoza: Joy, Sorrow, and the Feeling Brain.* Orlando, FL: Harcourt, 2003.

Damasio, Antonio. *The Feeling of What Happens: Body and Emotion in the Making of Consciousness.* New York: Harcourt, 1999.

Daw, Kurt. *Thought Into Action.* Portsmouth, NH: Heinemann, 2004.

Donnellan, Declan. *The Actor and the Target.* New York: Theatre Communications Group, 2002.

Downs, David. *The Actor's Eye: Seeing and Being Seen.* New York: Applause Theatre Book Publishers, 1995.

Easty, Edward Dwight. *On Method Acting.* New York: Ballantine, 1989.

Felner, Mira. *Free to Act: An Integrated Approach to Acting,* 2nd ed. New York: Pearson, 2004.

Funke, Lewis and Booth, John E. *Actors Talk About Acting.* New York: Random House, 1961.

Guskin, Harold. *How to Stop Acting.* London: Faber and Faber, 2003.

Hagen, Uta, with Frankel, Haskel. *Respect for Acting.* New York: Macmillan, 1973.

Hardwicke, Cedric and Brough, James. *Victorian in Orbit.* Westport, CT: Greenwood Publishing Group, 1972.

Harrop, John, and Epstein, Sabin R. *Acting With Style.* Englewood Cliffs, NJ: Prentice-Hall, 1982.

Hauser, Frank and Reich, Russell. *Notes on Directing.* New York: RCR Creative Press, 2003.

Hooks, Ed. *The Actor's Field Guide.* New York: Back Stage Books, 2004.

Hornby, Richard. *The End of Acting: a Radical View*. New York: Applause Theatre Book Publishers, 1995.

Johnstone, Keith. *Impro: Improvisation and the Theatre*. London: Faber and Faber, 1979.

Jory, Jon. *Tips: Ideas for Actors*. Hanover, NH: Smith and Kraus, 2000.

Jory, Jon. *Tips: Ideas for Directors*. Hanover, NH: Smith and Kraus, 2002.

Judith, Andrea. *Wheels of Life: A User's Guide to the Chakra System*. Saint Paul, MN: Llewellyn Publications, 1999.

Kearns, Michael. *Acting Equals Life: An Actor's Life Lessons*. Portsmouth, NH: Heinemann, 1996.

Lakoff, George and Johnson, Mark. *Metaphors We Live By*. Chicago: University of Chicago Press, 2003.

Lewis, Robert, and Clurman, Harold. *Advice to the Players*. New York: Theatre Communications Group, 1990.

Linklater, Kristin. *Freeing the Natural Voice*. New York: Drama Book Specialists, 1976.

Magarshack, David. *Stanislavski on the Art of the Stage*. New York: Hill and Wang, 1961.

Mamet, David. *True and False: Heresy and Common Sense for the Actor*. New York: Pantheon Books, 1997.

Manderino, Ned. *The Actor as Artist*. Los Angeles: Manderino Books, 1991.

Marowitz, Charles. *Stanislavski and the Method*. New York: Citadel Press, 1964.

Marowitz, Charles. *The Other Way: An Alternative Approach to Acting and Directing*. New York: Applause Theatre Book Publishers, 1999.

McGaw, Charles and Clark, Larry. *Acting Is Believing: A Basic Method*, 7th ed. New York: Harcourt, Brace Jovanovich, 1996.

Meisner, Sanford, and Longwell, Dennis. *Sanford Meisner on Acting*. New York: Vintage Books, 1987.

Mekler, Eva. *The New Generation of Acting Teachers*. New York: Penguin, 1987.

Miller, Bruce J. *The Actor as Storyteller*. Mountain View, CA.: Mayfield Publishing, 2000.

Moore, Sonia. *Training an Actor*. New York: Penguin, 1979.

Morris, Eric and Hotchkis, Joan. *No Acting Please*. New York: Perigee Books, 1977.

Nicola, James B. *Playing the Audience: the Practical Actor's Guide to Live Performance*. New York: Applause Theatre Book Publishers, 2002.

Olivier, Laurence. *On Acting*. New York: Simon and Schuster, 1986.

Pineo, Barry. *Acting That Matters.* New York: Allworth Press, 2004.

Pinker, Steven. *How the Mind Works.* New York: Norton, 1997.

Richardson, Don. *Acting without Agony: An Alternative to the Method.* Boston: Allyn & Bacon, 1998.

Rockwood, Jerome. *The Craftsmen of Dionysus: An Approach to Acting.* Glenview, IL: Scott, Foresman and Company, 1966.

Schiffman, Jan. *The Working Actor's Toolkit.* Portsmouth, NH: Heinemann, 2003.

Shapiro, Mel. *An Actor Performs.* Belmont, CA: Wadsworth, 1996.

Shurtleff, Michael. *Audition: Everything an Actor Needs to Know to Get the Part.* New York: Walker, 1978.

Smith, Raymond E. *An Actor's Workbook.* New York: Avery Publishing Group, 1989.

Spolin, Viola and Sills, Paul. *Improvisation for the Theater: A Handbook of Teaching and Directing Techniques.* Chicago: Northwestern University Press, 1999.

Stanislavski, Constantin. *An Actor Prepares,* trans. Elizabeth Reynolds Hapgood. New York: Theatre Arts Books, 1936.

Stanislavski, Constantin. *Building a Character,* trans. Elizabeth Reynolds Hapgood. New York: Theatre Arts Books, 1949.

Stanislavski, Constantin. *Creating a Role,* trans. Elizabeth Reynolds Hapgood. New York: Theatre Arts Books, 1949.

Stanislavski, Constantin. *My Life in Art,* trans. J.J. Robbins. New York: Theatre Arts Books, 1952.

Sternberg, Patricia and Garcia, Antonina. *Sociodrama: Who's in Your Shoes?* Westport, CT: Praeger Publishers, 2000.

Strasberg, Lee. *A Dream of Passion: the Development of the Method,* ed. Evangeline Morphos. Boston: Little, Brown, 1957.

Walter, Harriet. *Other People's Shoes.* London: Nick Hern Books, 1999.

Whelan, Jeremy. *Instant Acting.* Cincinnati, OH: Betterway Books, 1994.

Willet, John, ed. *Brecht on Theatre.* New York: Hill & Wang, 1964.

Williamson, Marianne. *A Return to Love: Reflections on the Principles of A Course in Miracles.* New York: Harper Paperbacks, 1996.

Wirth, Jeff. *Interactive Acting.* Fall Creek, OR: Fall Creek Press, 1994.

Witcover, Walt. *Living on Stage.* New York: Back Stage Books, 2004.

Yakim, Moni. *Creating a Character.* New York: Back Stage Books, 1990.

About the Author

David Hlavsa heads the Theatre Arts Department at Saint Martin's University, in Lacey, Washington, where he has been teaching acting, directing, and playwriting since 1989. He is the 2005–6 recipient of the University's Outstanding Teaching Award, and is currently serving a second term as Faculty President. His latest play, *Pack of Lies*, has been widely produced. He has a BA in English/Theatre from Princeton University and an MFA in Directing from the University of Washington. He lives in Seattle with his wife, Lisa Holtby, and their son Benjamin.

Index

Books from Allworth Press

Allworth Press is an imprint of Allworth Communications, Inc. Selected titles are listed below.

Acting Is a Job: Real Life Lessons about the Acting Business
by Jason Pugatch (paperback, 6 × 9, 240 pages, $19.95)

The Actor's Way: A Journey of Self-Discovery in Letters
by Benjamin Lloyd (paperback, 5 ½ × 8 ½, 224 pages, $16.95)

Letters from Backstage: The Adventures of a Touring Stage Actor
by Michael Kostroff (paperback, 6 × 9, 224 pages, $16.95)

Making It on Broadway: Actors' Tales of Climbing to the Top
by David Wienir and Jodie Langel (paperback, 6 × 9, 288 pages, $19.95)

An Actor's Guide—Making It in New York City
by Glenn Alterman (paperback, 6 × 9, 288 pages, $19.95)

The Art of Auditioning: Techniques for Television
by Rob Decina (paperback, 6 × 9, 224 pages, $19.95)

The Actor's Other Career Book: Using Your Chops to Survive and Thrive
by Lisa Mulcahy (paperback, 6 × 9, 224 pages, $19.95)

Improv for Actors
by Dan Diggles (paperback, 6 × 9, 256 pages, $19.95)

Acting—Advanced Techniques for the Actor, Director, and Teacher
by Terry Schreiber (paperback, 6 × 9, 256 pages, $19.95)

Promoting Your Acting Career: A Step-by-Step Guide to Opening the Right Doors, Second Edition
by Glen Alterman (paperback, 6 × 9, 240 pages, $19.95)

Acting that Matters
by Barry Pineo (paperback, 5 ½ × 8 ½, 240 pages, $16.95)

Movement for Actors
edited by Nicole Potter (paperback, 6 × 9, 288 pages, $19.95)

Please write to request our free catalog. To order by credit card, call 1-800-491-2808 or send a check or money order to Allworth Press, 10 East 23rd Street, Suite 510, New York, NY 10010. Include $6 for shipping and handling for the first book ordered and $1 for each additional book. Eleven dollars plus $1 for each additional book if ordering from Canada. New York State residents must add sales tax.

To see our complete catalog on the World Wide Web, or to order online, you can find us at **www.allworth.com.**